C000070263

Dancing with Jesus

THROUGH HURT, LOSS, AND
DISAPPOINTMENTS

Allison Broughton

TRILOGY CHRISTIAN PUBLISHERS

TUSTIN, CA

Trilogy Christian Publishers
A Wholly Owned Subsidary of Trinity Broadcasting Network
2442 Michelle Drive
Tustin, CA 92780

Dancing with Jesus

Copyright © 2022 by Allison Broughton

All Scripture quotations, unless otherwise noted, taken from THE HOLY BIBLE, NEW INTERNATIONAL VERSION®, NIV® Copyright © 1973, 1978, 1984, 2011 by Biblica, Inc.® Used by permission. All rights reserved worldwide.

Scripture quotations marked ESV are taken from the ESV® Bible (The Holy Bible, English Standard Version®), copyright © 2001 by Crossway Bibles, a publishing ministry of Good News Publishers. Used by permission. All rights reserved.

Scripture quotations marked MSG are taken from THE MESSAGE, copyright (c) 1993, 2002, 2018 by Eugene H. Peterson. Used by permission of NavPress. All rights reserved. Represented by Tyndale House Publishers, Inc.

Scripture quotations marked MEV are taken from the Modern English Bible, copyright © 2014 by Military Bible Association, published by Charisma House. Used by permission. All rights reserved.

Scripture quotations marked NLT are taken from the Holy Bible, New Living Translation, copyright © 1996, 2004, 2015 by Tyndale House Foundation. Used by permission of Tyndale House Publishers, Inc., Carol Stream, Illinois 60188. All rights reserved.

Scripture quotations marked NKJV are taken from the New King James Version®. Copyright © 1982 by Thomas Nelson. Used by permission. All rights reserved.

Scripture quotations marked TPT are taken from The Passion Translation®, Copyright © 2017, 2018, 2020 by Passion and Fire Ministries, Inc. Used by permission. All rights reserved.

All rights reserved, including the right to reproduce this book or portions thereof in any form whatsoever.

For information, address Trilogy Christian Publishing
Rights Department, 2442 Michelle Drive, Tustin, Ca 92780.

Trilogy Christian Publishing/ TBN and colophon are trademarks of Trinity Broadcasting Network.

For information about special discounts for bulk purchases, please contact Trilogy Christian Publishing.

Manufactured in the United States of America

Trilogy Disclaimer: The views and content expressed in this book are those of the author and may not necessarily reflect the views and doctrine of Trilogy Christian Publishing or the Trinity Broadcasting Network.

Library of Congress CataloginginPublication Data is available.

ISBN 978-1-68556-394-3

ISBN 978-1-68556-395-0 (ebook)

Dedication

This book is dedicated to my husband, children, and grandchildren—Bill, Billy, Shannon, Nicholas, Zachary, Mitchell, Logan, Troy, Olivia, and Donovan. My mom and dad—Barry and Barbara. Nicholas—we love and miss you, but we do not grieve like others without hope because we know you are in our future with Jesus. This is dedicated to the book you started before you left us. To the readers of this book—may you learn how to *Dance with Jesus* to find joy through hurts, loss, and disappointments. I tried hard to push through life and survive on my own, but I came to realize in time that *Dancing with Jesus* is resting in the dance of life He has for us.

Endorsements

As a pastor, I read things and think of others that it would help. I had the same mindset while reading *Dancing with Jesus*, but immediately the Holy Spirit revealed it was for me. Every word penetrated deep into my soul and pointed me to scriptures that I "knew," but I was refreshed in each one. This is not an ordinary book to be read casually, but it is meant to be read in your quiet space, allowing time for self-examination, meditation, growth, and healing.

A must-read...

Pastor Kaye Sims
Crystal Beach Community Church

Having lived through what quite possibly is the worst tragedy any parent could experience, Allison has learned to "dance" through each step of the pain and grief by keeping her ear close to the heart of Father God. Her firsthand account of the steps she took to come to her supernatural place of healing and find peace is a MUST-READ for anyone going through the hurt and pain of any tragedy. This book, which is chock-full of healing scriptures, will help the reader navigate through each step to discover and experience their own personal healing. I highly recommend this book as a teaching tool for any minister or person in charge of pastoral care as a tool to help guide others in finding healing and peace. *Dancing with Jesus* is a delightfully written, heartfelt guide to experiencing the ULTIMATE FREEDOM found in being in step with Jesus.

Susan and Charlie Mack Richardson

Love Never Fails Ministries

Dancing with Jesus will serve as a powerful tool for those who are dealing with grief. This book will walk one through the ways of learning to live with loss. The Word of God is shared throughout the book, which pours healing oil on the hurting. I have watched the author walk this path in her own life and come out restored. May you find healing and restoration through the journey of one who has gone before you.

Adina Keating, LMFT

If you are as busy as I am and really don't have time to read another book, don't even think about picking up *Dancing with Jesus*. The magnetism of Allison's writing skills will draw you in at the very beginning.

Most of us will never encounter the trial that Allison experienced. That is why it is intriguing to see what it is like to go through such an unexplainable tragedy as losing a child.

There's not a deeper valley to be trodden than the path Allison has faced. But as she articulately writes, Jesus Christ can and will, unmistakably, be the bridge over that chasm if you will let Him do so. The practical suggestions in this book are priceless for anyone going through indescribable adversity. I highly recommend you take the time to sit, read, and let this book transform the way you look at your life, your children, and your Savior.

Mike Hawkins
Author/speaker/real estate developer

This book, *Dancing with Jesus*, is not just a story but offers a collection of wisdoms and insights Allison gleaned as she walked her journey of healing from the incredible trauma of losing her son. Her story can offer you the inspiration and hope that you also can rise from the ashes of your own story of pain, even if the process is messy, is complicated, or even feels impossible. She shares how Jesus met her in very unique ways to free her from the heaviness of grief, how He spoke to the places of concern in her heart in only the way He can, and in these testimonies, you'll see the goodness of a kind God who, indeed, is near to the brokenhearted, and you'll be encouraged to continue reaching out to Him as you walk your own path of healing.

This book is broken into easily digestible sections that can also be pulled into your private time with the Lord, loaded with scripture and ready to feed your spirit. I pray that as Allison has been courageous in sharing her story, you would find comfort in her healing process and would be enriched as you eat of the fruit of her diligent pursuit of the Lord from those difficult days. Wherever you are in your journey of healing, I know this book will do exactly what Corinthians promises, in that you will "be comforted by the comfort she has received from Him," and that you then, too, will have testimonies and "fruit" of healing you can offer to those around you that testifies to God's goodness and faithfulness to bring beauty from ashes. Your journey is not over, God is not done, and Allison's story will be a spark to light hope in your heart as you continue putting one foot in front of the other in the strength and comfort the Holy Spirit brings. Blessings to you, dear reader!

Jenilee Samuel
Podcast host on Java with Jen Podcast and
executive pastor at Community Church, Orange, Texas

Acknowledgements

I would like to express my special thanks to my husband, Bill Broughton, for your love and support during the writing of this book, as well as for the encouragement and words of wisdom of close friends and people God placed around me. Thanks to my pastors, Nathan and Adina Keating, for standing behind me through the hardest journey of my life. And thank You, God, for never letting me go.

Contents

Introduction

Thank you for investing your time in reading Dancing with Jesus. I have prayed for each person who will read this book for healing over their lives. God directed my steps through the process of writing *Dancing with Jesus*. The name of the book was spoken to me through a pastor a year before the loss of our son Nicholas. He said, "I see you dancing with Jesus." At the time, I thought God meant I was going to be joyful all the time, just dancing along with Jesus. What I came to realize was that God was preparing me for a huge loss. He was going to teach me how to dance with Jesus, step for step, in order to be healed. He taught me that deep healing takes challenging work, but also that there is beauty in the way He blesses us through our perseverance. We will encounter the miracles God has for us when we stay in step with Him.

I pray you experience peace and joy beyond understanding and that God restores your heart as you read this book. Through reading this book, you will learn

how to lean your spirit into God's Spirit and experience
the way He wants to make you whole.

> But those who wait on the LORD
> Shall renew their strength;
> They shall mount up with wings like eagles,
> They shall run and not be weary,
> They shall walk and not faint.
>
> (Isaiah 40:31 NKJV)

CHAPTER 1

Why on Earth Did God Create Me?

> I have told you these things so that in Me you
> may have peace. In the world you will have
> tribulation. But be of good cheer. I have over-
> come the world.
>
> (John 16:33 MEV)

On the morning of March 5, 2019, our lives changed forever. It started out as a normal morning, but then our entire world turned upside down and in a split second came to a complete stop. Every morning, my youngest child, Mitchell, and I read a daily devotion before school. He is full of life with a sweet spirit, and another boy at baseball had been giving him a tough time in the dugout the night before. This was an ongoing problem with the same kid.

After nights of not sleeping well, I was exhausted with worry. I'd been fretting instead of giving the situation to God. Throughout the years, I have learned that suddenly waking up in the middle of the night meant that God was stirring me to pray. It was typically for my two older boys, who were twenty-one and twenty-four at the time. They were sweet-spirited, passionate young men, and they had each other for everything from an early age. I was always alert when God woke me up in the night, and I would pray for their safety. That night, there was no urging for prayer, only a nagging worry about how to manage this situation with Mitchell in baseball. Shortly after Mitchell and I had read our devotional that morning, the cell phone slid through my fingers onto the floor and the screen cracked, then half blacked out.

There was a knock at the door, which was unusual so early in the morning. Our middle child, Zachary, was standing outside at the front door, and I just knew. As I looked at him standing there looking at me, he didn't have to say a word; my heart instantly shattered. Nicholas, his older brother and best friend, had been killed at ten o'clock the evening before. His car had been hit by an eighteen-wheeler that came over a hill. Time stopped as I stared at Zachary standing in the doorway, and I needed this to be a bad dream. Zachary stared back at me, in so much grief. Mitchell kept saying, "No, it's just a dream, we are going to wake up," and my husband, Bill, started calling our friends. I could not breathe or see straight.

All I could think of was my Nicholas and how badly I wanted to go to him. I needed to throw up, and I wanted to die, but I couldn't. Nobody would let me go to him, and I could not understand what to do. I needed to go take care of him. One would think, as a momma, I would have felt something instantly, the moment it happened. And when I look back on that morning, I can see that my spirit already knew. The devil had distracted me all night with something else, and I let him. I carried a great deal of guilt because I thought I could have stopped the wreck before it happened. I told myself I should have heard God better that night and interceded in prayer. I had prayed all throughout this child's life and God had always intervened, but His intervention this time was to take Nicholas to heaven.

All that I could think and say was that "he has Jesus" over and over. The devil tried to tell me that he took Nicholas out, but God spoke to my heart, saying, "No, the devil did not win. My angels brought Nicholas to Me. The moment the truck hit Nicholas, he never suffered. My Son, Jesus, took his place on the cross, and He took his place behind the wheel." I knew in the moment of this horrible nightmare exactly where Nicholas was because he had received Jesus at summer camp when he was fifteen. His eyes changed that summer, and he carried himself differently. He had been made new. I needed to know where Nicholas was, but knowing He was with God helped me, to some degree, stay sane in that moment, but my heart was absolutely shattered.

Grief will make your whole body hurt, and I would lie on the cold floor because I couldn't get any lower. I thought it would just suck me up if I didn't move. The pain was so intense that only the cold floor or a bath full of water would help me disappear. Eventually, I realized I had to get up somehow and become present for my other two boys. It was a challenging thing—having to be strong for my children still on earth and also wanting to go to my child in heaven at the same time. Leaning on God's Word, I stood with one foot on earth and the other foot in eternity. My journey of healing with Jesus had begun. This was the deepest pain I had ever felt in my life, and only God could lead me to freedom and peace from there. I had so many questions: *Why did God decide to take him now? I've been praying over Nicholas and walking the floors of my house at all hours of the night, carrying my Bible close to my heart. How could my son, with his heart of fire and such a big personality, be gone?*

One Sunday at church before the accident, God had given me a vision of Nicholas walking on a stage, sharing the testimony of God's goodness in his life, but something extremely opposite had happened instead of what I saw. I was so confused, but my relationship with God was strong, and I knew if I let go of Him, I would explode from pain and not make it. When I asked God why, I would hear Him say over and over in my heart, My ways are not your ways. He tells us in His Word:

> For My thoughts are not your thoughts, nor are your ways My ways, says the LORD. For as the heavens are higher than the earth, so are My ways higher than your ways, and My thoughts than your thoughts.
>
> (Isaiah 55:8–9 MEV)

Before the tragedy, I stayed in the Word of God, which has helped me during the tragedy. His Word is our healing bread; it gives us nourishment daily. We feed our spirits when we study the Word, and the Holy Spirit helps us recall the words at the exact time they're needed. He has become my Best Friend, the only true Person whom I could lean on who was strong enough to hold me up. When horrible things happen to us in this life, we can lean on the wisdom of God and trust the Holy Spir-it to direct us. We can ask why, but we might not get the answer we're looking for. Still, God will give us peace if we ask,

We feed our spirits when we study the Word, and the Holy Spirit helps us recall the words at the exact time they're needed.

and we just need to trust that there is a reason for everything. As we are looking at Jesus face-to-face one day, I wonder if we will even care about the questions we had here on earth. There will be no more whys, and our hearts will be consumed with the love of Jesus. I will give Nick the biggest hug and I might not let him go! After all, we will have eternity to spend together.

I cannot ask God why anymore because I must trust that I did the best I could. I did my part, and I have allowed God to do His. He loves Nick, and He has taken care of him the way He felt was best. God knew something I didn't, and He had something better for Nick in heaven. So no more whys. Yes, there is a great deal of hurt and confusion, but no more whys. Instead, I started to pray, "God, if I'm going to be a strong mother and wife, then teach me and show me where Nicholas is. Tell me what he is doing and give me strength. Give me an eternity mindset and help me see with my Father's eyes."

A few weeks later, my closest friend invited me to a house church service with a small group of ladies. I was looking for healing and any type of relief from the intense pain. Anxiety attacks were hitting me, and my body was so heavy that it was hard to breathe. The Holy Spirit had put a strong urge in my spirit to go, and I knew the pastor who would be there might have something to say to give me relief. I went and sat down in a chair against the wall in the back of the room. The pastor was speaking the Word God had given her for that day, when she stopped suddenly and looked *straight at me.* I felt like the walking dead, like I barely existed sitting there.

"Allison!" she said. "God says you are going to heal so fast, and people are not going to understand. They are not going to understand how you are doing what you are doing." She walked up to me, sitting in my chair, then laid her hand on my head and said, "Spirit of torture, leave right now!" Immediately, the heaviness lifted off me, and I could breathe again. The spirit of torture she rebuked had been strangling me to the point that I could hardly think, but all of a sudden, I felt lighter. The ladies sitting there said I looked lighter suddenly. A stronghold had attached itself to me in the spiritual; it had found an open door of grief, and it held on to me spiritually, even physically affecting me.

A strong intercessor who walks close to God spoke to me next. She did not know how Nick had gone to be with Jesus, but she stated, "Your son was taken from the wreck by angels. He did not feel any pain as they lifted him above the wreckage. He looked down with joy in his heart, not with sadness." Something huge changed in my spirit right then. I had the beginning of healing and peace in my heart. I began to ask God what to do with the time I had left before I went to heaven. I then started the journey of what I call Dancing with Jesus. Just like a professional dancing couple, I danced with Him, and He did not take a step that I did not follow. I would like to take you with me on the journey of how the Holy Spirit has shown me, not just to heal daily but to have *victory* over what the devil thought he won.

Who Is God?

After the accident, every time I saw an eighteen-wheeler, I experienced full-blown anxiety. My thoughts were everywhere one morning as I was heading home from work, driving behind an eighteen-wheeler. On the back of the eighteen-wheeler, the words "*I AM*" were plastered across the back. These noticeable words grabbed my attention and reminded me of the story of Moses. When God commissioned Moses to deliver His people out of Egypt, Moses asked whom he should say had sent him.

And He said, "You will say this to the children
of Israel, 'I AM has sent me to you.'"
(Exodus 3:14b MEV)

As I let these words sink in, He gave me an inner peace once again, and I realized this might be a way that God was healing my fear. He is the I AM—exactly who I need Him to be. God has been so many things for me in my lifetime.

He has been my Savior, Rock, Comforter, Refuge, Shield, Strength, Peace, Father, Provider, and Living Water; I could go on and on. At that moment, I needed God to be every one of these things to me just so I could breathe. In our moments of need, He will be everything to us if we allow Him. He never left me during the hardest time of my life. Instead, I felt His presence deeper than ever before. When we feel an emptiness or a sense of panic, we can just call out to God. He will fill us with living waters of supernatural peace. He will show us a sign on the back of the truck, a redbird, a butterfly, a heart in the clouds, or a rainbow. He knows how to speak to each of us to heal our hearts. God is supernatural, and if we do not place Him in a box, He will lead us through our hurts.

I want to take us back, before the beginning of time.

> "I am the Alpha and the Omega, the Beginning and the End," says the Lord, "who is and who was and who is to come, the Almighty."
> (Revelation 1:8 MEV)

It's so hard to comprehend in our natural mind that God existed before time and that He is timeless. I love how Charles Spurgeon explains the relationship between God and time. He says:

All things are equally near and present to his view; the dis-tance of a thousand years before the occurrence of an event, is no more to him than would be the interval of a day. With God, indeed, there is neither past, present, nor future. He takes for his name the 'I AM'. (...) He is the I AM; I AM in the present; I AM in the past and I AM in the future. Just as we say of God that he is everywhere, so we may say of him that he is always; he is everywhere in space; he is everywhere in time.[1]

God is the *Creator* of everything; nobody created God. He created time, space, the galaxies, the solar system, water, grass, trees, and animals. Earth was created as a shadow of what God has made for us in heaven. For us to be able to survive on this earth, there had to be a perfect gravitational pull, as well as an oxygen-rich atmosphere. God is a strategic Planner, not impulsive; He is flawless, pure love, and a Spirit who does not have a physical body. When I was a child, I pictured God as a really big man that we could see. The Bible said the earth was His footstool, so I pictured Him sitting on a big throne wearing a crown and holding a huge staff in His hand, with His really big feet resting on the earth.

1 Charles Haddon Spurgeon, "God's Estimate of Time," The Spurgeon Center and Midwestern Baptist Theological Seminary, 2017, https://www.spurgeon.org/resource-library/sermons/gods-estimate-of-time/#flipbook/.

While the image in my young mind was literal, in this scripture, the use of "His footstool" means that God is victorious over heaven and earth.[2] The Word says He is a Spirit and omnipresent; how then can we contain Him in a box? Since God formed us, He can heal our broken hearts.

When Jesus sent the Holy Spirit to live in His believers, it became easier for us to receive healing. Because we have the Holy Spirit inside us, all we have to do is lean in with our spirits, rest, and believe He can heal us. Every work of creation and re-creation begins with the Holy Spirit. Before the foundations of the earth were formed, God's Spirit was hovering over the surface of the water, preparing to create.

> In the beginning God created the heavens and the earth. The earth was formless and void, darkness was over the surface of the deep, and the Spirit of God was mov-ing over the surface of the water.
>
> (Genesis 1:1–2 MEV)

God spoke everything into existence except for us. We are so loved by God that He formed us from dust and breathed His Spirit into us. This is so powerful!

---

2 Isaiah 66:1-2.

Then the LORD God formed man from the
dust of the ground and breathed into his nos-
trils the breath of life, and man became a living being.

(Genesis 2:7 MEV)

Our formed flesh is a timed exterior with a timeless
spirit, created to live on this earth. God created nothing
else like us! We are His children, made in His image,
and His Spirit lives in us.

For this reason we do not lose heart: Even
though our outward man is perishing, yet
our inward man is being re-newed day by day.
Our light affliction, which lasts but for a moment, works for us a far more exceeding and
eternal weight of glory, while we do not look
at the things which are seen, but at the things
which are not seen. For the things which are
seen are temporal, but the things which are
not seen are eternal.

(2 Corinthians 4:16–18 MEV)

God created the earth as a shadow of what He has
for us in heaven. We have beautiful mountains, oceans,
and skies. The sunset and sunrise over our oceans are
supernatural in their beauty and my favorite thing to

see. Imagine what the skies of heaven must be like if the earth contains so much beauty. We were created because God wants a relationship with us; He wants to spend eternity with us.

> *Our formed flesh is a timed exterior with a timeless spirit, created to live on this earth*

Why Does God Allow Me to Suffer?

A question that gets asked a lot is this: If God loves us so much, then why does He still allow us, His children, to suffer? Simply put, the answer is free will. The important thing to remember is that through all of our suffering, He has us in His hands, and God says He would never leave us or forsake us in our suffering.

Now the serpent was more subtle than any beast of the field which the LORD God had made. And he said to the woman, "Has God said, 'You shall not eat of any tree of the garden?'" And the woman said to the serpent, "We may eat of the fruit from the trees of the garden; but from the fruit of the tree which is in the midst of the garden, God has said, 'You will not eat of it, nor will you touch it, or else you will die.'" Then the serpent said to the woman, "You surely will not die! For God knows that on the day you eat of it your eyes will be opened and you will be like God, knowing good and evil." When the woman saw that the tree was good for food, that it was pleasing to the eyes and a tree desirable to make one wise, she took of its fruit and ate; and she gave to her husband with her, and he ate.

(Genesis 3:1–6 MEV)

In the Garden of Eden, Eve was tempted by the devil, disobeyed God, and enticed her husband to sin. Even if you haven't read the Bible, most people know who Eve is. She is blamed for sin, sickness, labor pains, demanding work, and death because she was deceived by the devil. He whispered in her ear that God was holding out on her. Any one of us could have been in Eve's position. I have even had the same heart before, just in a different situation. I was worried that I was missing out on something important and not at peace where God had me at the moment. We must learn to be with God in the season where He has placed us—not ahead and not behind. The anointing and

The anointing and grace from God are in the moment, not in the future or the past.

grace from God are in the moment, not in the future or the past. The anointing of God will not cover us if we are in sin or if we try to move ahead without Him. God created us to have free will, and He desires us to choose to worship and love Him. If He forced us to worship Him, we would not have been made in God's image. He would have made us as robots with computer chips. True friendship is not one-sided and forced.

The devil has been after us since the Creation because he wants to corrupt the love and plans God has for His children. He led and deceived some angels to rebel against God in heaven. He wanted the authority and the secrets that God would only share with us. The devil hates humanity, and he hates God. So, God threw the devil and his army of demons out of heaven.

> His tail drew a third of the stars of heaven, and threw them to the earth. The dragon stood before the woman who was ready to give birth, to devour her Child as soon as He was born.
>
> (Revelation 12:4 MEV)

In this verse, we see that the devil tried to take Jesus out over and over before the cross. He also wants to take out you, your children, and your grandchildren. He knows his time is ending, and he will do whatever he needs to do to separate us from God.

15

Even though the devil is out to get us, God loves us dearly and has not left us unprotected. He has left us with a complete suit of armor to defend ourselves and fight against the armies of darkness. He left us with armor and with a sword. Start every morning by putting on the armor of the Word of God. Just like a soldier places armor on before battle, we need the Bible (our armor) before our daily battles. When we have this in our hearts, it produces peace, truth, righteousness, faith, and hope. When we pick up and put on this armor daily, we can make it through the day and have victory over any hurts in our life.

God could have kicked the devil out of the Garden of Eden. He could have driven the devil away from Eve with a wave of His hand. He knew her flesh would be weak and that she would sin. He did not interrupt any of this because it was all part of His grandiose plan. The plan was not to stop at Eden. The plan was much more glorious than Eden. Eden was the beginning of the timeline of humanity. The new earth after Eden is the beginning of our eternity with God. He has plans for us that are so much lovelier than we could ever imagine.

Then I saw "a new heaven and a new earth." For the first heaven and the first earth had passed away, and there was no more sea. I, John, saw the Holy City, the New Jerusa-lem,

coming down out of heaven from God, pre-
pared as a bride adorned for her husband.
(Revelation 21:1–2 MEV)

We cannot see the whole picture as God sees it. We
can only see the moment of hurt or what we imagine
the future would be. This produces worry and fear,
which are the opposite of who God is. We need to focus
on the truth of what God says in His Word, no matter
what we see in the natural. He will place peace in our
hearts, even in tragedy, if we allow Him to. He promises
us a supernatural peace that only a supernatural God
can impart through His Truth and His Spirit. We cannot make sense of the fact that God knew and allowed
Eve to fall for the devil's tricks—that He allows terrible
things to happen to good people.

You see, the first Adam's disobedience resulted in
spiritual and physical death for us. Then, the death of
Jesus, the last Adam, resulted in eternal life for those
who repent and receive Him. Yes, it is all God's plan—
the plan of a timeless Father whose ways are not our
ways. Who brings good out of suffering and death because He is a good Father. When something horrible
and tragic happens in our lives, we must see it with His
eyes and heart. We must have faith that we are not seeing everything all at once.

Now faith is the substance of things hoped
for, the evi-dence of things not seen.
(Hebrews 11:1 MEV)

All of God's sons and daughters are waiting and
watching for something better that was promised to us.

We know that the whole creation groans and
travails in pain together until now. Not only
that, but we also, who have the first fruits of
the Spirit, groan within ourselves while ea-
gerly waiting for adoption, the redemption
of our bodies. For we are saved through hope,
but hope that is seen is not hope, for why does
a man still hope for what he sees? But if we
hope for what we do not see, we wait for it
with patience.
(Romans 8:22–25 MEV)

It is so hard to imagine that anything positive could
come out of pain when we are in the middle of the loss
of a loved one, a marriage, or a job. How can there be
any good in any of these situations at all? Well, there
might not be any good, but I trust that God allowed
them for a much bigger eternal reason than my mind or
heart can understand at the moment. We must go back
to the fact that God is the ultimate good and the devil is

the ultimate bad, and God did not cause our problems. We either walked into them with our bad judgment, or we were innocent and the devil moved among us as he did with Eve. God's purpose in these circumstances is necessary, and it only allows suffering for a good reason, one that we might not see in our natural state. We will see and understand more with time as we stay in God's Word.

> My soul clings to the dust; revive me according to Your word. I have declared my ways, and You heard me; teach me Your statutes. Make me to understand the way of Your precepts; then I shall contemplate on Your wondrous works. My soul collapses on account of grief; strengthen me according to Your word.
> (Psalm 119:25–28 MEV)

> Teach me, O LORD, the way of Your statutes, and I shall keep it to the end. Give me understanding, and I shall keep Your law and observe it with my whole heart.
> (Psalm 119:33–34 MEV)

With our armor on, God will sustain us through our suffering and restrict what Satan can do against us. God has already won the war, and because of the cross and eternity, so have we.

My brothers, take the prophets, who spoke in
the name of the Lord, as an example of suffering and patience. Indeed we count them
happy who endure. You have heard of the
patience of Job and have seen the purpose of
the Lord, that the Lord is very gracious and
merciful.

(James 5:10–11 MEV)

To me, endurance means a continuing lack of wavering during trials and difficulties. We must trust God
and believe what His Word says about us, no matter
what happens. We trust, because He promises us that
He will bring eternal goodness out of any earthly bad.

CHAPTER 2

How Can the Holy Spirit Help Us?

Every good gift and every perfect gift is from above and comes down from the Father of lights, with whom is no change or shadow of turning.

(James 1:17 MEV)

God gave me the gift of supernatural peace through the Holy Spirit after the loss of Nick. After the pastor prayed for me at the house church service, I was submerged in a wave of peace that had to be from God. I would still get hit with spells of grief, but I would say, "God, You take this from me. I can't do it." Then He would give me relief again. God will give us supernatural peace. First, we need to repent for any unbelief or any other sin that God lays on our hearts. Second, we must receive the gift of peace from God. Third, we must have faith that He gives it to us when we asked. Fourth, we must thank God for giving us supernatural peace. If somebody hands us a gift, we have to receive it, unwrap it, be blessed by it, and thank the Giver.

Read scriptures about peace and allow God to continue to speak into your life. Do not speak against what you received, because that will cancel out your gift of peace from God. What we speak matters, so be careful with your words.

> You will keep him in perfect peace, whose mind is stayed on You, because he trusts in You. Trust in the LORD for-ever, for in GOD the LORD we have an everlasting rock.
> (Isaiah 26:3–4 MEV)

I was in a close relationship with Jesus for years before Nick went to heaven. When I went down the wrong path in my twenties, God saved me and taught me through the Word of God. He led me to other spiritually mature people who taught me and helped me grow in God. In order to understand better who I was in Christ, I set aside time with God and studied the Bible every day. I would pray, sit still, and listen to what God would tell me. By doing all of this, I grew in God.

> So then faith comes by hearing, and hearing by the word of God.
> (Romans 10:17 MEV)

I began to crave my quiet time with God. It's amazing what He says to us when we get still. When we get still, we also allow God to minister to our hearts, and the power of the Holy Spirit overcomes us. We have a massive Superman inside of us, but some of us walk around as wounded casualties. The devil does not want you to know the greatness you carry as a child of God. The Holy Spirit is a Person, not a thing, and He is present. When I was a child, I thought the Holy Spirit was some type of floating Casper the Ghost. When Jesus died on the cross and went to be with God, He then sent the Holy Spirit to live in all believers.

> And I will ask the Father, and he will give you anoth-er Helper, to be with you forever.
>
> (John 14:16 ESV)

If a sinless Jesus had not sacrificed Himself on the cross for all of our sins, we would be forever separated from God. He was the only way for all of us at the same time to receive the Holy Spirit and keep us connected to God eternally. "[The] Holy Spirit is not only a Being having another mode of

We lean in with our spirit and connect to God instantly through the Holy Spirit.

existence, but He is Himself a Person, with all the qualities and powers of personality. He is not matter, but He is substance."[3] He is literally a Person living inside of us. When we realize this, we can understand how we can receive instant comfort and peace. We lean in with our spirit and connect to God instantly through the Holy Spirit.

> Likewise, the Spirit helps us in our weaknesses, for we do not know what to pray for as we ought, but the Spirit Him-self intercedes for us with groanings too deep for words.
>
> (Romans 8:26 MEV)

I started to practice speaking to the Holy Spirit like I would speak to another person. In the morning, I would say, "Good morning, Holy Spirit!" Over time, we became intimate, and I can hear Him in my heart clearly. That's the relationship we want to have. When I read my Bible, the Holy Spirit points out the Father's heart to me. When I'm still in the presence of God, His glory comes over me, and He tells me the secrets of His heart. The Holy Spirit is my best friend. In the Old Testament, God removed His hedge of protection from the Israelites because they were living in continuous sin, but Daniel listened, trusted, and obeyed God. God revealed hid-

---

3 A.W. Tozer, *How to Be Filled with the Holy Spirit*, Reprint (Moody Publishers, 2016).

den things to Daniel, and the favor of the Lord rested
on him.

> "He changes times and seasons; he deposes
> kings and raises up others. He gives wisdom
> to the wise and knowledge to the discerning.
> He reveals deep and hidden things; he knows
> what lies in darkness, and light dwells with
> him. I thank and praise you, God of my ances-
> tors: You have given me wisdom and power,
> you have made known to me what we asked
> of you, you have made known to us the dream
> of the king."
>
> (Daniel 2:21–23 NIV)

We should be able to hear God because of the Holy
Spirit. In the Old Testament, before Christ, God chose
people to whom He would speak because of how their
hearts were turned toward Him. Now if we reach for
God with a repentant heart, we can hear the Holy Spirit.
It is truly up to us how close we become to God. When
He died on the cross, Jesus made it possible for us to ap-
proach God directly and for the Holy Spirit to descend
upon us.

> In Him you also, after hearing the word of
> truth, the gospel of your salvation, and after

believing in Him, were sealed with the promised Holy Spirit, who is the guarantee of our inheritance until the redemption of the purchased posses-sion, to the praise of His glory.

(Ephesians 1:13–14 MEV)

The Holy Spirit is our inheritance until Jesus comes back for us. The Holy Spirit protects and gives us discernment. We should never go anywhere without the presence of the Holy Spirit. The anointing of the Holy Spirit on us can have an effect on the spirits of those around us. Recently, I walked into a store, and the Holy Spirit came alive inside of me with *boldness*. The anointing made every hair on my body stand up. The cashier behind the counter became very rude and seemed agitated. I thought, *Okay, I'm just going to give her these clothes calmly.* When there are spirits in people that are not of Jesus (demonic), they will react badly to the Spirit of Jesus (the Holy Spirit). Our spirits were clashing, and hers was in an argumentative state. This was not from God. We are set above, not below, our circumstances with the Holy Spirit. It is definitely a spiritual war. We have the means to react to adversity with calmness and authority.

We are set above, not below, our circumstances with the Holy Spirit.

There can be a great deal of confusion when it comes to the Holy Spirit and different beliefs about Him. The only place to find the truth is in the Word of God. One aspect of this confusion is whether we lose the presence of the Holy Spirit because of our sin. The Word of God says we are all sinners and not perfect. We all sin, whether we tell a lie, gossip, or steal, and even in our hearts, when we think badly of another.

Listen, it's a heart matter, and the closer we become to the Holy Spirit and walk in a repentant heart, the harder it is to commit these sins. But what if we slip up? Does God get mad and take away His sealed Spirit from us? Look at Abraham, Isaac, David, Peter, and so many others in the Bible. They sinned, but they had repentant hearts, and they are all in heaven now and doing amazing things, I'm sure! What does the Word of God say?

> For by grace you have been saved through faith, and this is not of yourselves. It is the gift of God, not of works, so that no one should boast.
>
> (Ephesians 2:8–9 MEV)

Our salvation has nothing to do with anything we do; rather, it is based on faith. Jesus did all the hard work so that we wouldn't have to. He took our sins on the cross, and we receive Him in our hearts. We are redeemed by the blood of the Lamb. No extra work from us can get us to heaven. In the same way, we cannot unseal the Holy Spirit from ourselves by sinning. His love is not circumstantial, and His gifts are not irrevocable. If you grew up in a house where the love you received was circumstantial, it is hard to comprehend this. To understand this is to understand the depth and the heart of our Father's love for us. Let's look at God's strategic plan for the Israelites and us in the last days. This is a big section of scripture, but I wanted to point out how God hardened Israel's heart just for a time, until the fullness of us, the Gentiles, came through Jesus.

> For I do not want you to be ignorant of this mystery, brothers, lest you be wise in your own estimation, for a partial hardening has come upon Israel until the fullness of the Gentiles has come in. And so all Israel will be saved, as it is written: "The Deliverer will come out of Zion, and He will remove ungodliness from Jacob"; "for this is My covenant with them, when I shall take away their sins." As concerning the gospel, they are enemies for your sake, but as regarding the election, they are beloved for the sake of the patriarchs. For the gifts and calling of God are irrevo-cable. For just as you once were disobedient to God, but have now received mercy through their disobedi-

ence, so these also have now been disobedi-
ent, that they also may receive mercy by the
mercy shown to you. For God has imprisoned
them all in disobedience, so that He might be
merciful to all.

(Romans 11:25–32 MEV)

God made a covenant with Israel's patriarchs that
the Deliverer will come out of Zion and all Israel would
be saved. In our natural eyes, it looks like a huge por-
tion of Israelites in the Middle East were against Jesus,
but it's all part of God's plan. Eventually Israel will receive the same mercy that has been shown to us. God's
plan and purpose will be fulfilled. The point here is that
they could not break a covenant made by God around
2071 BC. We cannot break a covenant God made with
the blood of Jesus when He sealed in us the Holy Spirit.
God, the Son, and the Holy Spirit in one—the complete
Triune of love fulfilled is sealed in you.

One thing I know for sure is that I could not have
gotten this far in my journey without the peace and love
of the Holy Spirit. I'm living proof that He is alive and
works through me because He is my best friend. His
presence is like a glorious blanket of peace that I feel,
and you can, too. Imagine the glory our loved ones feel
in heaven if we are allowed to feel the small bit we experience here. If they were given a choice, I believe they

would not want to leave God's glory. Let's look at the fruit our Spirit produces because of the Holy Spirit living in us.

The Fruit of the Spirit

I grew up in church and accepted Jesus in my heart when I was ten. There was no radical burning-bush encounter like Moses had, but I had an understanding that Jesus died for me and I needed to have Him in my heart to get to heaven. Just like several others who are new to the Kingdom, that was where my understanding and personal responsibility stopped. I was safe to make it into heaven, but I never grew or realized my identity in Christ. My identity was in anything that was of interest at the moment, and when that interest inevitably fell through, so did my identity. We are walking around, lost and broken, looking for people, places, and things to fulfill our identity. All of these can, and will eventually, let us down. The amazing thing is, if we are believers, the fulfillment is not far away. It is right inside of us. The Holy Spirit will help us have supernatural peace and a knowledge of belonging to something so much bigger than us.

God will bring to the table the desires of our hearts when we stop relying on the natural world and start relying on Him.

Make God the utmost delight and pleasure of your life, and he will provide for you what you desire the most. Give God the right to direct your life, and as you trust him along the way you'll find he pulled it off perfectly! He will ap-pear as your righteousness, as sure as the dawning of a new day. He will manifest as your justice, as sure and strong as the noon-day sun.

(Psalm 37:4–6 TPT)

When we allow God to direct us, we also allow the Holy Spirit to re-create our spirits so we can produce the fruit of the Spirit. What is the fruit of the Spirit, exactly? It is Christlike behavior that is the natural result of growing closer to God and developing the mind of Christ.

But the fruit of the Spirit is love, joy, peace, patience, gen-tleness, goodness, faith, meekness, and self-control; against such there is no law. Those who are Christ's have crucified the flesh with its passions and lusts. If we live in the Spirit, let us also walk in the Spirit.

(Galatians 5:22–25 MEV)

The closer we become to Jesus, the more of the mind of Christ we have. You can look at the fruit a person produces to get an idea of their daily walk with Jesus. This can help you realize the depth of relationship to have with others if you want to go into business with somebody or be in a serious relationship with them. The more we allow the Holy Spirit to re-create our spirit, the more peace we have while walking in the world. I'm not saying we are going to be okay with everything that happens in the world around us, but we will carry the peace of Jesus within us. When we have Jesus, we're no longer of this world. We are passing through, from birth to death, as visitors. The Holy Spirit helps us visit this world with peace and allow others to see how Jesus wants us all to live. The cares of the material world are no longer as important as the cares of the eternal spirit. The grudges and offenses we thought were so important become trivial.

The devil of this world wants you to think the lies of this world are the truth. He hopes to keep you from seeing the real truth of Jesus' love and forgiveness. When we produce the fruit of the Spirit, we are allowing Jesus (the Vine) to flow through us (the branches). Look at this beautiful scripture and imagine His blood pumping through to you to keep you beautiful and strong on the inside and out.

"I am the true vine, and My Father is the vine-dress-er. Every branch in Me that bears no

fruit, He takes away. And every branch that
bears fruit, He prunes, that it may bear more
fruit. You are already clean through the word
which I have spoken to you. Remain in Me, as
I also re-main in you. As the branch cannot
bear fruit by itself, un-less it remains in the
vine, neither can you, unless you re-main in
Me."

(John 15:1–4 MEV)

Fruit starts as a seed and grows and matures into a
sapling and then a tree that bears fruit. So we, too, start
as baby Christians and gradually mature as we grow in
Jesus. We stay connected to Jesus, and He helps us mature. Our fruit becomes healthy and beautiful.

When I accepted Jesus in my heart as a child, I didn't
grow in the Word. I went to church, Sunday school,
and camps. I just never got to know Him in a personal
way. The fruit never grew in my life. I would get angry and rebel in many ways, even as a grown woman.
When Mitchell (our youngest son) was born, his lungs
were not developed, and the doctors could not guarantee healing. I fell to my knees and cried out to Jesus
for his healing. Bill and I begged and prayed. I told God
I would get my children in church, and I would serve
in church, if He would please heal Mitchell. Mitchell's
lungs grew and developed every day for nine days. The

number nine in the Bible signifies completeness, or finality! I stuck with my promise when Mitchell was strong enough to go to church. I wrapped him up, and we all went to church. I went to our local Christian bookstore and bought a women's study Bible. When I started reading the Bible in my thirties, the words poured into my heart and mind. I started thinking in a separate way and looking at things differently. My heart softened, and I had a deeper love for others. The Holy Spirit was slowly transforming my spirit to become like Jesus. I was producing the fruit of the Spirit organically because of my relationship with Jesus.

Along with the fruit of the Spirit, we also have the gifts of the Spirit available to us. *The word of wisdom, word of knowledge, faith, gifts of healings, working of miracles, prophecy, discerning of spirits, various kinds of tongues, and interpretation of tongues all by the same Spirit.*[4] As important as these are for the growth of the Church as a whole, it is better to have the fruit of the Spirit with these, rather than just having the gifts of the Spirit. Without the love and grace of Jesus, we can end up causing harm rather

> *Without the love and grace of Jesus, we can end up causing harm rather than benefiting God's Kingdom.*

---

4 1 Corinthians 12:8-10, MEV.

than benefiting God's Kingdom. I have met people who flow in the gifts of the Spirit but who have no love. It's really sad, because that will push others away from God.

> If I speak with the tongues of men and of angels, and have not love, I have become as sounding brass or a clanging cymbal. If I have the gift of prophecy, and understand all mysteries and all knowledge, and if I have all faith, so that I could remove mountains, and have not love, I am noth-ing. If I give all my goods to feed the poor, and if I give my body to be burned, and have not love, it profits me nothing.
>
> (1 Corinthians 13:1–3 MEV)

We grow by ingesting the Word of God daily. We become less like children and more like mature brothers and sisters in Christ in time.

Paul was speaking to the Corinthian church about how they were acting according to their flesh more than their spirit. Christians have a higher call to come out and be separate, not to live like the rest of humanity.

> Brothers, I could not speak to you as to spiritual men, but as to worldly, even as to babes in Christ. I have fed you with milk and not with

solid food. For to this day you were not able to endure it. Nor are you able now, for you are still worldly. Since there is envy, strife, and divisions among you, are you not worldly and behaving as mere men?

(1 Corinthians 3:1–3 MEV)

The heart surgeon, the Holy Spirit, comes in and performs heart surgery as we grow in His Word. Sometimes I regret I did not have a better relationship with Jesus earlier in my life. Then God reminds me that without my history; I would not empathize on the other side of this as well. God has a plan and purpose for each of our lives. God already knew we would make the wrong decision that day, and He also knew when we would accept Him in our hearts. There is no skipping forward in the process of building our character (fruit). We are a work in progress, and we will never be fully perfect until we get to heaven.

When we accept things in the past and in the moment as the way it is supposed to be, our next breath becomes easier over time. Acceptance and forgiveness in the present become easier. When things seem out of sorts, I look at the situation and say, "Is everybody and everything okay, right at this moment?" Usually, the answer is yes. God can work with this because you are now in the moment with Him. He can start building His fruit in your life to produce it now and in the future. We do not know the future, but we can let it go and place it in God's hands. God tells us not to remember the former things so that He can do a new thing. I look at this with a natural mindset and think, *How could I forget my son and accept that it is meant to be this way? All I have of him are my memories, and I will not forget my past!*

God does not intend for me to forget Nicholas or for you to give up what you hold so precious to your heart. But He does want us to change how we view our past. Look at it with an eternity mindset, the way He sees it. God is timeless, and He sees it all in one picture, wrapped up in a beautiful mess of redemption.

> "Stop dwelling on the past. Don't even remember these former things. I am doing something brand new, something unheard of. Even now it sprouts and grows and matures. Don't you perceive it? I will make a way in the wilderness and open up flowing streams in the desert."
> (Isaiah 43:18–19 TPT)

The Holy Spirit is a gentleman, and He waits for us, so we have to invite Him to re-create our spirits, minds, and souls. He will take all bad and painful memories and right now start to create good (fruit) from them.

The devil does not want you to heal and produce fruit. He wants to keep you in the guilt of your past. A Christian with no fruit is a useless Christian who is no help to anybody. But God has already won this war on earth. God's power in your life will help make it so much easier to bear the fruit of the Spirit. Let's look at what the Holy Spirit can do in your life if you allow Him.

The Purpose of the Power of the Holy Spirit

> For this reason I bow my knees to the Father of our Lord Jesus Christ, from whom the whole family in heaven and earth is named, that He would give you, according to the riches of His glory, power to be strengthened by His Spirit in the inner man, and that Christ may dwell in your hearts through faith; that you, being rooted and grounded in love, may be able to comprehend with all saints what is the breadth and length and depth and height, and to know the love of Christ which surpasses knowledge; that you may be filled with all the fullness of God. Now to Him who is able to do exceedingly abundantly beyond all that we ask or imagine, according to the power that works in us, to Him be the glory in the church

and in Christ Jesus throughout all generations, forever and ever. Amen.

(Ephesians 3:14–21 MEV)

The fruit of the Spirit and the power of the Holy Spirit have different purposes. The fruit is the Holy Spirit
re-creating our spirits so we can produce love and the
nature of Jesus. The Holy Spirit's power is shown when
God comes over us with His presence.

I love God's presence. He is like a warm, cozy blanket
of peace wrapped all around me. I never want to go a
day without His presence.

He alone is my safe place; his wrap-around
presence al-ways protects me. For he is my
champion defender; there's no risk of failure
with God. So why would I let worry paralyze
me, even when troubles multiply around me?

(Psalm 62:2 TPT)

With the fruit of the Spirit and God's presence and
power, we have everything we need to walk in the world.
The fruit and the power have two distinct functions,
but both are needed to have peace and share the love
of Christ. We do not have to have one without the other. The fullness of the Holy Spirit helps us surpass our
knowledge and our wisdom when we speak with others.

Let me tell you a beautiful story about God's love. When I was in my late thirties, I began an in-depth study of precept Bible studies at my church. God was using this to draw me in, and I was really getting to know His personality. His Word truly became my bread. All I wanted to do was read and study it, and all the worldly things became very empty.

Jesus said to them, "I am the bread of life. Whoever comes to Me shall never hunger, and whoever believes in Me shall never thirst."

(John 6:35 MEV)

Everything in the Bible is true, and if we are confused about anything, all we need to do is ask Him to explain it in a way we can understand. I had Kay Arthur books, videos, commentaries, and a class full of like-minded women in my church who loved Jesus. Through God's Word, the Holy Spirit began to re-create my spirit. My character and personality started to change, but I still held on to things that became a part of me. I had a difficult time trusting others, and I kept them at arm's length. I tried, but I just never felt good enough to be accepted. I didn't think they would really like the real me. I still kept seeing my old self and not my new self in Christ.

God loves us so much that He doesn't want us to stay this way. He knew I needed more of Him to understand

His love for me and others. As Paul wrote in Ephesians, I needed to know the love of Christ that surpassed my knowledge and to be filled with the fullness of Him. After five years of studying all the different books of the Bible, teaching Sunday school to the little ones, and going to the women's prison with a ministry, I finally had a radical encounter with

In one second, God placed me in a deep sleep and gave me heart surgery.

Jesus. I was asked to visit a church with a friend. All it takes is one touch from Jesus, and you will be forever changed. Something inside me kept urging me to go to the front of the church. Now I know that "something" was the Holy Spirit. At the front was a woman who was praying for people. She laid her hand on my head, looked in my eyes, said something about Jesus, and the next thing I knew, I was on the floor, apparently for a while. In that one second, God placed me in a deep sleep and gave me heart surgery. He breathed in me like He did in Adam, and my dry bones came alive.

> So the LORD God caused a deep sleep to fall on Adam, and he slept. Then He took one of his ribs and closed up the place with flesh.
>
> (Genesis 2:21 MEV)

This was actually the first anesthetic done when God put Adam to sleep for surgery. God created it and later gave man the idea.

What He did for me, no human therapy or self-help book could do. He strengthened my spirit, gave me a new outlook, and filled me with new knowledge and a complete fullness of Him. The colors of everything around me brightened so much that I could not get enough of His creation. There was also an instant peace and love for others that I had truly never had before. I had always had to work extra for these things. The scriptures that I already fell in love with once seemed to come off the page, speaking straight to me in a way they never had before. Jesus filled me with the Holy Spirit's power that evening, and I would never be the same. He can, and He will, do the same for you. The Holy Spirit is a promise from God.

> "But when the Counselor comes, whom I shall send to you from the Father, the Spirit of truth who proceeds from the Father, He will bear witness of Me."
>
> (John 15:26 MEV)

I don't want to take away from the amazing fact my uncle was praying for me to know more of God that same evening. This is proof we can be praying in faith for others in another city or across the world, and God hears us. It's important to stand in faith that God will answer us. Another fitting example is my grandmother's prayers for me to grow closer to God when I was growing up. Her prayers set things into motion for me, and they are being answered even after her death. We set things in motion from the time we wake up to the time we go to sleep in the physical and spiritual realms.

> *We set things in motion from the time we wake up to the time we go to sleep in the physical and spiritual realms.*

How great are His signs, and how mighty are His wonders! His kingdom is an everlasting kingdom, and His dominion is from generation to generation.

(Daniel 4:3 MEV)

We have the authority of Christ to set prayers into motion. God gave us this authority, and He wants us to use it to cover our family for generations. Continually pray for your children and grandchildren. Remember, God is timeless, and He is not working only in your time zone. Your prayers are being heard, and with your faith, they will be answered, even generations later, just as my grandmother's prayers are now touching generations of those she has prayed for. I have been able to see my prayers moving through my children and grandchildren. Some nights I would read scripture while placing Nick's name in it and walk the floor. He loved Jesus and had the biggest heart, but as many of us do, he struggled with the hurts of this world. There are struggles in our DNA we cannot help that come from the blood of our ancestors carried down from generations. It's really not our fault that we were born with those chains. That's why it's important to speak out that generational curses be broken and that the blood of Jesus is passed down instead.

One evening I was on my knees on the floor at the front of the church. A lady I didn't know and have never seen since spoke this word from God to me: "God says, 'But you gave Him to me, and I have him.'" She didn't even know I had lost my son just two weeks before. She was right. I did give Nick to God many times in his life. One day at the beach, I found a pink rock, and imagining it was Nick, I threw it out in the ocean, saying, "He is Your child, God." I would have to do things like this because I would worry myself sick about him. I said, "I give Nick to You, Father, and I know You love him so much. You do a much better job taking care of him than my worrying does." For God to have Nick in heaven now is definitely not what I meant by that prayer, but I came to terms that it was His way of not letting go of our boy and instead protecting him from the devil's schemes with that truck. Nick was also protected from the unforeseen future that God knew of and I didn't. It hurt to hear what she said, but it helps tremendously to know that God is protecting Nick in heaven. God was giving her secret knowledge of Nick to give to me for the healing of my heart. God was being gracious to my heart by speaking these words to me through her that night. We know our prayers were heard for Nick because, even in our hurt, God has him, and I will get to see Nick again.

The overwhelming presence and power of the Holy Spirit have wrapped me up through these past two years, to keep my heart safe during our tragedy. This power and presence of Christ are available for all His children. I'm closer to my heavenly Father than ever before in my life. In the book of Acts, when the disciples were filled with the Holy Spirit, they had a new boldness to preach and heal with the authority of Christ. After the evening of my "heart surgery" by God, I began to walk with Jesus with a hunger in me that no other person or thing could fill. When I went back into the prison ministries, I would pray with others and God would impart them with His presence. Words started to flow from me that were words of encouragement and words of their future from God. He filled me so I could share the cross, His love, and His healing with a boldness and an impartation of His presence to others. The fullness of the Holy Spirit was given to me through the laying on of hands. And when I began laying on hands on others, the Holy Spirit was then imparted to them.

> Therefore I remind you to stir up the gift of God, which is in you by the laying on of my hands.
>
> (2 Timothy 1:6 MEV)

Walking in the power of the Holy Spirit is especially important while raising children and being a spouse. You have so much more supernatural grace, wisdom, and knowledge with your family because of God's power gifts in you. When we pray for our children, the Holy Spirit leads us in exactly what to pray for, and when we are confused, He gives discernment behind the situation. My husband and I have prayed for our children and grandchildren with the authority and power of Christ. He shows us, with discernment and knowledge, what sicknesses to speak against. We are in a spiritual war. Why would God leave us here in the devil's world powerless? We do not have to wake up another day being a victim of his schemes anymore. Fear, sickness, depression, and grief are not ours to carry because Jesus carried them on the cross. Yes, we will get hit with these things because we are living life, but He will always give us a way out. The way out is so much easier when we have the power of Christ to take authority over them.

With God's power and His Word, He will teach us how to hear, discern, and walk out our healing by listening closely to Holy Spirit.

> *With God's power and His Word, He will teach us how to hear, discern, and walk out our healing by listening closely to the Holy Spirit.*

Now concerning spiritual gifts, brothers, I do not want you to be ignorant. You know that you were Gentiles, carried away to these dumb idols, however you were led. Therefore I make known to you that no one speaking by the Spirit of God says, "Jesus be cursed!" And no one can say, "Jesus is the Lord," except by the Holy Spirit. There are various gifts, but the same Spirit. There are dif-ferences of administrations, but the same Lord. There are various operations, but it is the same God who operates all of them in all people. But the manifestation of the Spirit is given to everyone for the common good. To one is given by the Spirit the word of wisdom, to another the word of knowledge by the same

Spirit, to another faith by the same Spirit, to
another gifts of healings by the same Spirit,
to another the working of miracles, to another prophecy, to another discerning of spirits,
to another various kinds of tongues, and to
another the interpretation of tongues. But
that one and very same Spirit works all these,
dividing to each one individually as He will.

(1 Corinthians 12:1–11 MEV)

We should not go one more day without the *power* of
the Holy Spirit. Jesus said we would do more than Him
when He walked on this earth.

"Very truly I tell you, whoever believes in me
will do the works I have been doing, and they
will do even greater things than these, because I am going to the Father."

(John 14:12 NIV)

Jesus walked in all the gifts of the Spirit because He
is one with God. We walk in the gifts of the Spirit as He
wills—and that might be one or more gifts.

I would like to show you how the Holy Spirit can
teach us, in all areas of our lives, to be a victor, even in
the worst moments of our life. He will help us heal and
function again in a world where we were hurt. If you

have accepted Jesus in your heart, then you have already been sealed with the Holy Spirit. If you have never received the power of the Holy Spirit, and you would like to repeat this prayer, have faith and believe that He will do what you have asked. Just breathe and receive in the quiet of His presence.

> Dear Jesus, please fill me to overflowing with Your Holy Spirit so that I can love You more, follow You more close-ly, and have greater power to tell others about Your love and salvation. Amen.[5]

---

5 "Holy Spirit Power," The Family International, 2022, https://www.thefamilyinternational.org/en/faith-foundations/the-basics/holy-spirit-power/.

CHAPTER 3

Clearly Hearing Holy Spirit in the Noise

There's a private place reserved for the lovers
of God, where they sit near him and receive
the revelation-secrets of his promises.

(Psalm 25:14 TPT)

A deeper relationship comes with spending more
time with God, not just reading a devotion quickly in
the morning and moving on with your day. That's better than nothing, but that's not a good relationship.
We need to spend more than thirty minutes a day with
somebody to get to know their personality and experience intimacy with them. Spend time in God's Word
and be aware of what He is showing you daily. God created us with six senses, and He loves to show Himself
to us through them—hearing, touching, tasting, smelling, seeing—along with a knowing in our spirit. This
is also how He helps us understand and notice what is
happening in the spiritual world. That is why the devil

tries to dull our awareness and get us to follow counterfeit senses. Counterfeits are the worries of this world and things in the natural that we place above God.

The devil also wants to keep our senses dulled by both good and bad busy work. As long as we are busy, he doesn't care. This will keep us confused and unable to know the truth about dancing with the flow of Jesus.

> "My sheep hear My voice, and I know them, and they fol-low Me."
>
> (John 10:27 MEV)

We will know God's voice if we try to hear Him and spend more quality time with Him. If we don't know His ways very well, we can be deceived by the worldly things around us. If we are placing God first, everything else will make more sense. We will not be disturbed or in fear of the same things that others are afraid of all around us. The Holy Spirit covers our spirits and gives us peace beyond understanding. We can also taste the goodness of God spiritually. I can walk into a room with God's gift of discernment and taste either the sweetness of God or the foulness of sin.

> How sweet are Your words to the taste of my mouth! Sweeter than honey to my mouth!
>
> (Psalm 119:103 MEV)

Is there injustice on my tongue? Cannot my
taste discern pernicious things?

(Job 6:30 MEV)

> *When we are not suited up spiritually, we can walk into a situation defenseless and not even be aware that we are emptyhanded.*

The devil will try his best to dull your sense of taste of spiritual things. If we are constantly reaching for things that are not of God, the senses God created our bodies to experience will be dulled. When we are not suited up spiritually, we can walk into a situation defenseless and not even be aware that we are emptyhanded. Walking into warfare without armor or a sword is not smart. Yes, Jesus is always with us, and no, He never leaves us. How, then, will you discern where and what to do at the time if you can't hear Him? We stay aware by trying our best to keep our minds and hearts pure.

God always makes his grace visible in Christ, who in-cludes us as partners of his endless triumph. Through our yielded lives he spreads

the fragrance of the knowledge of God everywhere we go.

(2 Corinthians 2:14 TPT)

God can smell a good offering or a bad offering from
the intent of our hearts. Do we carry the sweet fragrance
of Christ or a rotten smell wherever we go?

It's the same with the spiritual sense of smell that
God gave us. It is so much more than just smelling in
the natural. There is a sweet smell when Jesus is in the
room. An example is when people come to my work,
they just love it there. It's full of God's Spirit and has
a cozy feel to it. You can just smell the sweetness of
Christ. People like to come to just sit and visit.

The father of Publius in the Bible was sick in bed:

His father was sick in bed, suffering from fever and dys-entery. Paul went in to see him
and, after prayer, placed his hands on him
and healed him.

(Acts 28:8 NIV)

A heavenly transfer of healing can be given through
a touch from one person to another. When I pray for
healing, Jesus anoints my hands with heat and transfers
healing to others.

One gift God has given me, which I am still growing in humbly every day, is seeing visions. The key word
here is humbly. Never place the gifts of God before
a relationship with Him. We should practice having
an awareness of what He is showing us with childlike
faith. That means trusting what He is showing us. God
wants to heal our hearts, and if we allow Him to do so,
He will. I've received healing through the visions God
has given me. They are beautiful movielike visions, in
color. One was of Nicholas, and he was on all fours on
the ground, playing with children beneath a big, beautiful tree. The children would run and hop over him in a
game of leapfrog, and I could see and feel the joy of all of
them. I said, "Father, if they are experiencing such joy
in heaven, please help me feel joy also like them while
I'm still here on this earth." Every time God shows me
a vision, I gain a little more peace and healing in this
broken heart.

One of my favorite stories in the Bible is when the
king of Syria plotted the capture of Elisha. Elisha's servant saw the horses, chariots, a great army surrounding
their city, and he was afraid. The mountain was full of
horses and chariots of fire from God, and they were on
Elisha's side. Elisha asked God to show his servant what
was truly behind them and open his spiritual eyes.

"Don't be afraid," the prophet answered.
"Those who are with us are more than those

who are with them." And Eli-sha prayed, "Open his eyes, LORD, so that he may see." Then the LORD opened the servant's eyes, and he looked and saw the hills full of horses and chariots of fire all around Elisha.

(2 Kings 6:16–17 NIV)

We have an army of angels on our side, and they want to help us—we just have to believe.

There is also the knowing sense. You just know that you know that you know. God will give you a definite knowing, as if He had said it audibly to you. This is a strong discernment about something. The more we listen and trust, the more He will show us.

But when the Spirit of truth comes, He will guide you into all truth. For He will not speak on His own authority. But He will speak whatever He hears, and He will tell you things that are to come.

(John 16:13 MEV)

If our thoughts are clouded by the world of social media and TV, those will be the things we think about. Try to stay away from these things and think about the truth. Listen to worship music, plug in to the Word of God, and grow in a deeper relationship with Him so you can learn to flow with Jesus in the way He is leading the dance. The closer our relationship with our Father is, the more aware we will become of what He wants to show us.

Our Father is full of grace, and it's okay to seek to hear Him with childlike, humble faith. One thing God will never do is ask us to do something against His Word. It takes effort on our part to establish a relationship with other people, and it also takes effort to get to know our heavenly Father.

One afternoon, before picking Mitch up from school, I heard God speak to my heart. It was one of the first times I experienced this. I didn't hear an audible voice, but I felt an urgency and a knowing in my spirit. This is a powerful sense I have that God uses to speak to me personally. I know this, because the more I listen to the way He speaks to me, the more He trusts me. I then hear Him to a greater extent, as close friends do. That afternoon, I was driving on our main street in town on my way to pick my son up from school. I heard, *Stop and speak to the man at the bus stop.* I shrugged it off and decided that was not a good idea because I might be late.

The farther I drove past him, however, the more uncomfortable I felt. I said, "Okay, fine, what should I do? Give him money?" I turned my car around, parked, put some money in my pocket, and walked across the parking lot to the bus stop. I had no clue what was going on, but I immediately felt better, as I was doing what

I was told. Every step became more peaceful, and I had an easier time breathing. When I looked at the man, he seemed a little startled. Then I heard God say, *Tell him that I see him, and I love him.* I said, "God says that He sees you, and He loves you." I looked at the man, and he looked at me, and then I went back to my car with joy in my heart. I had allowed God to use me as a vessel. I still don't know why, but God wanted me to give that man this message for a reason. We need to hear God, do what He says, and leave the outcome in His hands. You are a vessel and should allow Him to use you. By allowing His Spirit to flow, we will experience the glory and testimony of His love and be a blessing to others. To do this, we need to trust with childlike faith.

Childlike Faith

> For by grace you have been saved through faith, and this is not of yourselves. It is the gift of God, not of works, so that no one should boast.
> (Ephesians 2:8–9 MEV)

Everybody has faith in something. We have faith that the light bulb will turn on when we flip the switch. Incredibly, we have faith that other drivers on the road will stay in their own lane. God imparted the gift of faith to us when we were formed in our mother's womb. He also gave us the free will to choose what and whom we will have faith in. If all we watch is the news, then soon our faith will be in the news. When we read the Bible, our faith begins to grow deeper and stronger, and the more we will get to know God.

> So then faith comes by hearing, and hearing by the word of God.
>
> (Romans 10:17 MEV)

He wants us to give all our cares to Him. It takes practice to do this, especially if we normally run the show in our daily life. We can practice by daily giving the small things to God. It becomes much easier to allow God to take care of the bigger things when we grow accustomed to letting Him take care of the smaller things. Start small, by giving your time to God. An example is, "God, You have the next five minutes of my day. They are Yours to do with what You want." Pretty soon, we are accustomed to flowing and dancing to Je-

It becomes much easier to allow God to take care of the bigger things when we grow accustomed to letting Him take care of the smaller things.

sus' steps instead of our own. The more dependent we become on God, the more independent and self-confident we actually become in this world. It's the opposite of what somebody who likes control might think. When we learn to let go and let God, our faith grows, and so does our peace.

Mary, the mother of Jesus, had an amazing, childlike faith. What a wild encounter she experienced, and what a great example of total trust! God sent an angel to tell Mary that He was going to impregnate her by the Holy Spirit, and she was going to carry the Savior of the world.[6] Most of us would have discussed with our friends if having a baby at that moment was a proper time for us or whether it really was a word from God. Not Mary; she accepted what God said and allowed Him to manage the rest.

> The angel answered her, "The Holy Spirit will come upon you, and the power of the Highest will overshadow you. Therefore the Holy One who will be born will be called the Son of God. Listen, your cousin Elizabeth has also con-ceived a son in her old age. And this is the sixth month with her who was declared barren. For with God nothing will be impossible." Mary said, "I am the servant of the Lord. May

---

6 Luke 1:26-56.

it be unto me according to your word." Then the angel departed from her.

(Luke1:35–38 MEV)

Mary endured the looks from other people, and Joseph nearly walked away from her. She was close to being stoned to death for the false accusation of having premarital sex. It didn't matter—the looks and whispers of others—she continued to trust God. She trusted through Jesus' life all the way to the foot of the cross as her son hung on it and afterward.

> Near the cross of Jesus stood his mother, his mother's sis-ter, Mary the wife of Clopas, and Mary Magdalene. When Jesus saw his mother there, and the disciple whom he loved standing nearby, he said to her, "Woman, here is your son," and to the disciple, "Here is your mother." From that time on, this disciple took her into his home.
>
> (John 19:25–27 NIV)

Mary didn't understand most of the time, but she trusted God with complete abandonment and a childlike faith. Mary heard God and rested on the promise that He was doing His part. Because of her faith, Mary experienced miracles and the firsthand love of our Father. It didn't end the way she thought it would, standing at the cross grieving her son. She probably asked God why He would let the crucifixion happen after all of the promises she'd been given She didn't understand the full plan, but she was able to experience the miracle of Jesus coming back. He was able to tell His mother that it was not over yet—it was just beginning. They had won the battle, and they would be together again in eternity. Even though it was horrible, it occurred for a reason. We don't always understand the purpose in the middle of our hurt or loss, but we must just keep doing the next right thing, which is our part in life. We take our hands off the reins and have faith that God will cover the rest.

Only after giving control to God can we experience the healing and miracles of Jesus. Healings and miracles happen when we have childlike faith, like Mary. When we have faith in the supernatural way, God moves in this world. If we give control to God because of our faith in Him and His Word, then we must believe everything in it—this and the fact that

> *The world is a shadow of the eternity God created for us.*

there are angels and demons all around us. Just like Elisha prayed for God to open the servant's eyes, we should pray for God to open our *spiritual* eyes and stop being so skeptical. This world is a shadow of the eternity God created for us. The spiritual existence all around is extremely busy. It's sad because many people just believe what they see in the natural. They keep God in a small box and stay discouraged. When there is a message for me from God—on an eighteen-wheeler or a heart in the sky—I know, without a doubt in my heart, it is from God, because I have childlike faith. The closer we get to the Holy Spirit, the easier it is to notice when He gives us an inner nudge.

God knows our hearts and knows exactly what to do to heal us. We have to trust that He will heal our hearts in a different way than He would our friends'. We are all created with different personalities, so doesn't it make sense that we would receive healing in separate ways? That's why it's important to get to know your Healer and His Word. God and His Word never change, but He knows exactly what His children need.

When my youngest was playing baseball, Nick didn't make it to all the games he wanted to. He missed a game, and the next week, during Mitchell's baseball game in the evening, Nick was in the wreck. We had to continue with the games for Mitchell, even though it was so hard. That baseball season, Mitchell thrived and made remarkable plays. My family came together, and it was our saving grace to go and watch the games. It was a time of healing and restoration for our family, and God was all in it. I could feel the angels all around us. Mitch's team went all the way to the playoffs, and it was amazing to watch the joy in Mitchell, a joy we had never seen before when they won. We all felt in our hearts that heaven itself was pulling for the Yard Goats that season.

The next baseball season, Nick was pulling for us again. He was making up for not coming to the games. Nick's nickname had White Buffalo. He was half white (from me) and half Native American (from his father). His father's side of the family is from the Umpqua tribe of Oregon. When Nick passed, some of his friends wore bracelets that said White Buffalo. His brother Zachary had a white buffalo head circled inside a dreamcatcher tattooed on his arm. So buffalo meant something special to everyone. The next season, the coach who picked Mitchell named his team the Bisons. One morning on the way to work, I was praying for Mitchell to have good teammates and coaches like he'd had the last season. When I stopped at a red light, a big eighteen-wheeler pulled up beside me with the word BISONS written so big that it filled the entire side of the truck. My heart leaped with joy. God saw the needs of our family, and heaven was pulling for us again.

Through the sport of baseball, God was healing our hearts and showing us He had us. It was one of the last connections we had with Nick. Nick was showing up at the games. I could just see him in heaven talking to God and the angels, saying, "Let's show them who we are rooting for and that we can see them." That season we had a great coach, and he moved Mitchell to third base. We won every game but one, and we won the championship again. We had a great cloud of family and friends cheering us on in heaven. We persevered that baseball season, and we still do every day, with the confidence that heaven has our backs. It reminds me of this verse:

> Therefore, since we are encompassed with such a great cloud of witnesses, let us also lay aside every weight and the sin that so easily entangles us, and let us run with en-durance the race that is set before us.
>
> (Hebrews 12:1 MEV)

We all have angels and loved ones who are cheering for us. When you receive heavenly kisses, accept them and know who sent them to you. They will bring a smile to your face and healing to your heart.

He Is Close to the Brokenhearted

We are made in God's image, which means we are like Him. We have the same characteristics, personality, and emotions He has. Have you ever heard that you are just like your mother, father, or grandparents? We might not have ever met them, and we might have been raised by somebody else. However, we could have the same expressions or laugh because of our family's DNA. Most importantly, we have our Creator's DNA.

> Then God said, "Let us make man in our image, after our likeness..."
>
> (Genesis 1:26 MEV)

This is beautiful because we are made in the image and likeness of the Father, the Son, and the Holy Spirit. Our emotions and personality come from our heavenly Father. He has kindness:

> For His merciful kindness is great toward us, and the faith-fulness of the LORD endures forever.
>
> (Psalm 117:2 MEV)

He has love:

> "For God so loved the world that He gave His only begot-ten Son, that whoever believes in Him should not perish, but have eternal life."
>
> (John 3:16 MEV)

He has empathy:

> For we do not have a High Priest who cannot sympathize with our weaknesses, but One

who was in every sense tempted like we are,
yet without sin.

(Hebrews 4:15 MEV)

He has anger:

The wrath of God is revealed from heaven
against all un-godliness and unrighteousness of men, who suppress the truth through
unrighteousness.

(Romans 1:18 MEV)

He has sorrow and grief:

Jesus wept.

(John 11:35 MEV)

If my heavenly Father, who made me to be like Him,
experiences anger, joy, and grief, shouldn't it be okay
for me to experience these emotions? Many people are
ashamed or fearful to show any emotion. However, if we hide our emotions, we will never heal. I was scared to let go totally. I didn't want to talk about the wreck or go to the gravesite at first because it would put me in panic

> *To grieve is like losing yourself and fearing you will never make it back.*

attack mode. I knew a lady who said she screamed in her car at the top of her lungs after her child passed. I couldn't scream because I was scared I would shatter. If I moved too fast or was too loud, then I felt the pain even more. To grieve is like losing yourself and fearing you will never make it back. Behind every emotion of God is love. Love is behind His holy anger because of His children's sin. Love is the motivation behind a parent's anger toward our children when they continually make bad choices. Love is behind God's grief for us. We grieve because we love. God wants us to grieve and experience emotions because He can touch us in our vulnerability.

He also says that if we draw close to Him, He will draw close to us.

> Draw near to God, and He will draw near to you.
>
> (James 4:8 MEV)

He is at the door knocking—we just have to open it and invite Him in. God says He is close to the broken-hearted, and it's true.

> Listen! I stand at the door and knock. If anyone hears My voice and opens the door, I will come in and dine with him, and he with Me.
>
> (Revelation 3:20 MEV)

God is here knocking but look at what He says. He says, "Draw near to Me first and open the door so I can come in and dine with you." When I was able to walk back into the church after Nicholas's death, it was scary because everything seemed so big around me. I had found comfort in my home, my couch, and my Bible. God told me it was time to go back to church. He always gives a gentle nudge for the next step, and I listen.

I went back to church, and when the worship music came on, I lifted my arms. With heavy arms and a broken heart, I raised them. When I drew near to God, His presence overcame me. I reached for Him like a child would a parent, and I was overcome with waves of peace. There is healing and victory in God's presence. There is a story in the Bible about Moses holding his hands up in victory on a hill. He praised God through the battle, and when his arms grew heavy, his friends held them up for him. The enemy was defeated, and the Israelites won because Moses praised God until the victory was manifested in the natural.

> Now when Moses held up his hand, Israel prevailed, but when he let down his hand, Amalek prevailed. But Moses' hands became heavy. So they took a stone, and put it under him, and he sat on it. And Aaron and Hur supported his hands, one on one side, and the other on

the other side. And his hands were steady until the going down of the sun. So Joshua laid
low Amalek and his people with the edge of
the sword.

(Exodus 17:11–13 MEV)

Your breakthrough begins when you start to trust
God through the storm and raise your hands to Him in
victory, because no matter what, the devil is defeated.
Keep praising Him and when it becomes hard, do it
anyway. The Holy Spirit is our Helper; just like Moses'
friends helped him, ask Him to help you. We don't have
to look far or hard. God wants to help us and give us
comfort. The Bible tells us that God is close to the brokenhearted. When I was lost in grief from losing Nick,
I knew exactly what this scripture meant. I have never
been as close to God as I have been in the last two years.

The LORD is near to the broken-hearted, and
saves the contrite of spirit.

(Psalm 34:18 MEV)

God spoke to me, permitting me to grieve, remain
home for a time, and stay in His Word. There were
days, even now, when I would sit in silence and read
God's Word. We talk, and I would cry or just be in His
presence.

My brothers, take the prophets, who spoke in the name of the Lord, as an example of suffering and patience. Indeed we count them happy who endure. You have heard of the patience of Job and have seen the purpose of the Lord, that the Lord is very gracious and merciful.

(James 5:10–11 MEV)

God restricts what Satan can do against us, and He sustains us through our suffering. In the Old Testament, there were a certain number of days given to grieve, and then the mourner would journey forward. Some mourned seven days and some thirty days.

> *God restricts what Satan can do against us, and He sustains us through our suffering.*

Professional mourners were also required. They would play instruments, mourn loudly, not leave the house, and quit all grooming and entertainment. They would just read the Torah. God called for them to mourn, and He takes it seriously. There is a healthy way to mourn. Everybody grieves differently, but we should grieve with the hope of Christ. Now because of Jesus, we do not grieve like others—we grieve with hope. We have hope because of the cross of

Christ and eternity. I once watched an older man walk by me at a restaurant and thought to myself, *Not that long ago, that man was a little boy.* We age quickly and die, and our spirits leave and go to heaven if we believe. Life is truly a vapor. We live with passion for the day that God gives us.

> But I would not have you ignorant, brothers, concerning those who are asleep, that you may not grieve as others who have no hope. For if we believe that Jesus died and arose again, so God will bring with Him those who sleep in Jesus. For this we say to you by the word of the Lord, that we who are alive and remain until the coming of the Lord will not precede those who are asleep. For the Lord Him-self will descend from heaven with a shout, with the voice of the archangel, and with the trumpet call of God. And the dead in Christ will rise first. Then we who are alive and remain shall be caught up together with them in the clouds to meet the Lord in the air. And so we shall be forever with the Lord. Therefore comfort one another with these words.
>
> (1 Thessalonians 4:13–18 MEV)

As I shared with you earlier, God also comforts and heals us with dreams and visions. Since the scribing of the Old and New Testaments, and all the way till today, God has given visions and dreams to people. When we receive a dream or vision from God, it will always line up with the Word of God. I like to write them down and later go back and read over them. The first vision I had of Nick was the night after I found out he had died. When the grief would become unbearable, I would turn all the lights off in my bathroom and get in the bathtub with water to the top. I asked, "God, please show me what he is doing." I closed my eyes and saw Nick sitting at a small wooden table in heaven. I saw my uncle who had passed away, and Nick was sitting across from him. Nick had one hand down on the table, with his head back as he was laughing really big. There were people standing all around the table, but all I could see were their legs. Nick was beautiful—no lines of worry, just a smooth, young face. There is truly so much waiting for us after this life. I started to cry and felt some of the heaviness lift off my spirit.

My heavenly Father is close to the brokenhearted. I sensed that heaven must be just a veil away, as if I could place my hand in the air, and it would go through the veil of the spiritual. There are no tears, sadness, or anger in heaven. The people there can see us only with joy as they cheer us on. Another vision I had of Nick was with him on a bridge with two children. They looked like school-age, around seven or eight years old. On one side of the bridge was a green field with wildflowers and some beautiful trees, but mostly a green field. On the other side of the bridge was a beautiful, bright golden castle, but you had to walk a little bit to get to it. There was a stream under the bridge. Nicholas was pointing to the biggest, most blue butterfly I have ever seen. I asked God, "Who are these children, and why is Nick now always with children?" God spoke in my heart, telling me, very clearly, there are many children in heaven, and they need mentors. Nicholas is mentoring children in heaven. This fits Nicholas perfectly, since he always had a soft spot for kids, and he wanted to be a history teacher at one point. Nick had a teaching gift, and he is now being used in the Kingdom of heaven. How can that not bring healing to a momma's heart?

Maybe you don't trust that what you are seeing is from God, or you feel it's just your imagination. The closer you become to God, the more that trust develops, and you will understand that He loves to talk and sit with you. God desires us to sit with Him and just be okay with Him. I was in the Spirit and asked God what Nicholas was doing. I saw Jesus and a bench swing by the water. Jesus asked me to sit beside him. We sat together, and I just rested beside Him. He just wants us to rest with Him. He loves us so much. To receive healing from God, we need to be willing to be obedient and trust Him.

CHAPTER 4

Rewards of Obedience

If you are willing and obedient, you shall eat the good of the land.

(Isaiah 1:19 MEV)

Obedience sounds harsh to this generation. Our culture today is a feel-good, don't-offend-others generation. There is only a small number who read, follow, and obey the Word of God. However, obedience to Christ is freedom from bondage. He removes the yoke of this world from our necks.

"Come to Me, all you who labor and are heavily burdened, and I will give you rest. Take My yoke upon you, and learn from Me. For I am meek and lowly in heart, and you will find rest for your souls. For My yoke is easy, and My burden is light."

(Matthew 11:28–30 MEV)

We're in bondage when we are not obedient to God but obedient only to our fleshly desires. When we're in bondage, it feels like we're emotionally yoked by the world, handcuffed, and thrown behind bars. We might not be physically walking around handcuffed, but our minds, spirits, and souls are chained up. When we follow the plan and outline that God has shown us in the Bible, the chains start breaking off. The sensation of repeatedly running into the wall and going in circles will stop.

My husband loves all sports. The Bible, in a way, reminds me of a playbook the coaches use.

> A playbook is a collection of a football team's plays and strategies, all compiled and organized into one book or binder. A team's playbook may be separated into sections for offensive plays, defensive plays and specials teams, or they may have separate playbooks for each discipline.[7]

When we follow the Bible, we are given defensive plays, offen-sive plays, and strategies all in one book. We do not have to look far to know how to live our life well. We blame the devil for every difficulty, when most

7 "What Is a Playbook in Football? Definition and Meaning," SportsLingo, 2022, https://www.sportslingo.com/sports-glossary/p/playbook/.

of the time, it is the natural consequence of our bad decisions. We follow our manmade god (our made-up rules) and not the true God of the Bible. When we become comfortable with the sins of the world, we lose our identity in Christ. Then we make God in our own image, and we no longer grow in His complete image.

> *When we become comfortable with the sins of the world, we lose our identity in Christ.*

If any of you lacks wisdom, let him ask of God, who gives to all men liberally and without criticism, and it will be giv-en to him. But let him ask in faith, without wavering. For he who wavers is like a wave of the sea, driven and tossed with the wind. Let not that man think that he will receive anything from the Lord. A double-minded man is unstable in all his ways.

(James 1:5–8 MEV)

We place Him in our little box and wrap Him up. Leaning into God and trusting Him does not always feel safe. It can, in fact, feel a little scary and messy. When we lean in, trust, and obey Him, He will always come through.

Only 24 percent of Americans think the Bible is the literal Word of God.[8] The world is under the control of the devil until Jesus comes back.

> We know that we are children of God, and that the whole world is under the control of the evil one.
>
> (1 John 5:19 NIV)

The devil covers our eyes and our ears to the truth of God. The only One who can uncover our eyes and ears is God, and the only way to God is found through Jesus.

> Jesus said to him, "I am the way, the truth, and the life. No one comes to the Father except through Me."
>
> (John 14:6 MEV)

Jesus is the Word made flesh.

> The Word became flesh and made his dwelling among us. We have seen his glory, the glory of the one and only Son, who came from the Father, full of grace and truth.
>
> (John 1:14 NIV)

---

8 Lydia Saad, "Record Few Americans Believe Bible Is Literal Word of God," Gallup, Inc., 2017, https://news.gallup.com/poll/210704/record-few-americans-believe-bible-literal-word-god.aspx.

The only way to know the true God is through Jesus, the Living Word. Light and truth are in Jesus, and we who carry the light and truth will walk in obedience and freedom.

> Again, Jesus spoke to them, saying, "I am the light of the world. Whoever follows Me shall not walk in the darkness, but shall have the light of life."
>
> (John 8:12 MEV)

The more darkness there is in this world, the more our light shines and can be seen. There has never been a more opportune time to let your light shine. We are in the darkest hour ever, and God placed us here for such a time as this. To make this time count, we have to be obedient to God's Word. Obedience means to hear, listen, and obey. To hear God's Word and act accordingly is being submissive to God. The word obey in the Old Testament means "to hear."[9] In the New Testament, the word *obey* also means "to trust."[10] A person's obedient response to God's Word is a response of trust or faith. So, to really hear God's Word is to obey God's Word.

> Now therefore, if you will faithfully obey My voice and keep My covenant, then you shall be

---

9 Trent C. Butler, Editor, "obedience," in *Holman Bible Dictionary*, 1991, https://www.studylight.org/dictionaries/eng/hbd/o/obedience.html.
10 Ibid.

My special posses-sion out of all the nations,
for all the earth is Mine.

(Exodus 19:5 MEV)

If we yield to, hear, and trust God's Word faithfully, then we will be His special possession out of all the nations. In simple terms, He has your back, and you will have favor!

This doesn't mean things will go our way all the time. Jesus says we will have tribulation on this earth.

"I have told you these things so that in Me you may have peace. In the world you will have tribulation. But be of good cheer. I have overcome the world."

(John 16:33 MEV)

During times of trouble, God has us surrounded with His wraparound love and protection. When people who walk obediently with Jesus lose family and friends to death, I've heard them say, "We are in pain, but at the same time, we can feel God's peace." How exactly can this be? God will place His hands on our hearts and hold us together.

One morning I was on the treadmill at the gym, and God showed me a beautiful picture of a heart with shattered black lines all through it. He then filled His red blood all through the black lines, and His blood held the heart together. How beautiful this image was! God tells us in His Word that if we stay close to Him, then He will stay close to us.

> Draw near to God, and He will draw near to you. Cleanse your hands, you sinners, and purify your hearts, you dou-ble-minded. Grieve and mourn and weep. Let your laugh-ter be turned to mourning, and your joy to dejection. Humble yourselves in the sight of the Lord, and He will lift you up.
>
> (James 4:8–10 MEV)

I've had people ask me how to hear God. He is our Father and wants to interact with us. God is not far away at all. He is inside of us, and if we stay humble and teachable, we will learn to hear Him. One way to hear Him is through Scripture. It speaks to us. This is called a rhema word (alive and active), and it is prophetic. It will resurrect, heal, deliver, comfort, test, and give hope. I have seen people running from prophetic speaker to prophetic speaker to give them answers, but they never open the Word of God for themselves. We have to be careful if a spoken prophetic word does not line up with God's Word. A true prophetic word will heal our hearts and give us hope. I've had many prophetic words spoken over me, including one that told me the name of this book. The Bible tells us to heed the prophets, but we should use godly wisdom in doing this, and we will find this wisdom in God's Word. Also, God does speak audibly. I have heard God's voice in my sleep three times. It was the same deep, clear voice, and it woke me up instantly. Once He said my name and woke me up. I didn't know better at the time, and I should have said, "Speak, Lord, for I hear You." This is what Samuel said to God when He woke Samuel up. God wakes me up and speaks names clearly to me, and I have learned that I don't have to know why in order to pray for them.

Another way of hearing God is when He speaks to you in your dreams. The Holy Spirit will tell you if it's a "God dream" or not. When you clearly remember a dream, even five years later, as if it happened last night, God is ensuring that you will remember it. A dream from God is orderly, and He will never give you chaos or fear. He may warn you in a dream, but it is to protect you and others. I've had many of them. The reason God speaks to us is to help us understand the deeper things of God and to help oth-

> *The reason God speaks to us is to help us understand the deeper things of God, and to help others understand.*

ers understand. Ask God what to do with the dream, and He will give confirmation in our hearts when it's time to share or act on it. I'm still holding on to dreams of prophecies because He hasn't allowed me to release them to anyone else yet. God's dreams are clear and detailed. They are always clear in your mind and can be remembered as if you just had them. Dreams may take years to manifest, or they can have an immediate manifestation. We need to have faith in what God is showing us and, even if we cannot see evidence of it, that it is spiritually in the works. The Holy Spirit will tell us when and how to be obedient to these dreams.

Also, God will give us visions. The kind I have is like a movie playing in front of me. I've had two visions with my eyes open and the others with my eyes closed. During the open-eye visions, everything in the natural world around me disappeared. The Holy Spirit gives us these visions for hope and strength. Keep praying through what God promised and trust the process. One open-eye vision was of Nicholas on a stage with tattoos up and down his arm. He was preaching and sharing his testimony. I thought, *Okay, God, I can see the plans You have for Nicholas.* Then, three years later, God brought Nicholas home to be with Him. I said to my pastor's wife, "This is not what I saw. I know what God showed me." But I knew His ways are not my ways. In trusting Him through the pain, God will give us supernatural peace.

Now I can see it was the plan for Nicholas that I had in the vision. God didn't fall through; our side fell through. Sometimes, when we choose another route other than God's ways, the consequences are hard. Nicholas is sharing his testimony onstage with the saints and angels in heaven now instead of on earth. His younger brother, Zachary, has been getting tattoos up and down his arms. This is something new for Zachary. I'm resting in the fact that God is not done with these boys of mine, and the mantle is being handed down to Zachary that was prophesied over Nicholas. In the Bible, we read that when Elijah was taken by the Lord, his mantle was passed to Elisha.

> Then Elijah took his robe and rolled it up and struck the water, and it was divided from one side to the other. Then the two of them crossed on dry ground. And as they were crossing, Elijah said to Elisha, "Ask for something, and I will do it for you before I am taken away from you." And Elisha said, "Let a double portion of your spirit be upon me." He said, "You have asked for a difficult thing, but if you see me when I am taken from you, it will happen to you. If not, it will not." As they continued walking and talking, a chariot of fire and horses of fire separated the two of them, and

Elijah went up by a whirlwind into heaven. Elisha was watching and crying, "My father, my father, the chariot of Israel and its horsemen!" And he did not see him again. Then he grabbed his own clothes and tore them in two pieces. He picked up the robe of Elijah that fell from him, and he returned and stood on the bank of the Jordan. And he took the robe of Elijah that fell from him, and struck the water, and said, "Where is the LORD, God of Elijah?" When he had struck the water, it parted from one side to the other, and Elisha crossed over. When the sons of the prophets who were at Jericho saw him from far off, they said, "The spirit of Elijah rests on Elisha." And they came to meet him and bowed down to the ground before him.

(2 Kings 2:8–15 MEV)

God laid Elijah's mantle on Elisha.

God speaks to us in the natural through numbers, signage, and people. Our spirits will quicken when something is meant for us. One evening, I missed Nicholas so much. A wave of grief was coming over me while I was driving to my friend's house for a get-together. I had tears running down my face, and I was hurting terribly. I said, "God, please tell me where exactly Nick is, please, and tell me what he is doing." The song *21 Years* by Toby Mac immediately came on the radio. It was a song that Toby Mac wrote about losing his son. A part of the song says, "Is it just across the Jordan or a city in the stars?"[11] Just as he sang the word "Jordan," I looked to my right as I passed a street sign I had never noticed before—it said "Jordan." I broke down. God was telling me again that He had Nicholas. He never tires of my questions, and He always comforts me.

We have to be aware of our surroundings and turn down the noise of the world. "Crossing the Jordan is a turning point on the way to Freedom. The waters of the Jordan represent freedom from oppression, breakthrough, and deliverance."[12] God told me that Nicholas is free, and I had a breakthrough. The Holy Spirit highlights things just for us. Our spirits will see something that's normal in the natural, but we know God pinpointed it just for us.

Lastly, God is in the quiet, still, small voice inside of us. Tune out the world, be still, and listen. God wants us to quiet down and just be with Him. He desires and cherishes our time. In the Bible, Elijah had to do just that after his victory over the Baal worshipers. He was worn out after the victory. After a godly victory, the

---

11 "21 Years," lyrics by TobyMac, 2020, Songtext Co., 2022, https://songtexte.co/en/tobymac-21-years-lyrics-1769b8.

12 FIRM Staff, "Crossing the Jordan River and Its Spiritual Significance," FIRM: Fellowship of Israel Related Ministries, 2020, https://firmisrael.org/learn/crossing-jordan-river-spiritual-significance/.

devil brings confusion against us because he is angry. After Elijah's victory, Jezebel, the evil queen, said, "I'm going to kill you, Elijah," so he ran and hid. God sent an angel to refresh him. When we lean into God's presence, He will give us new oil. He refreshes us with His touch. Then God spoke and gave Elijah directions. He was obedient, even though there was fear because Elijah knew there were blessings and victory in the obedience.

> *God wants us to quiet down and just be with Him. He desires and cherishes our time.*

Then he lay down under the bush and fell asleep. All at once an angel touched him and said, "Get up and eat." He looked around, and there by his head was some bread baked over hot coals, and a jar of water. He ate and drank and then lay down again. The angel of the LORD came back a second time and touched him and said, "Get up and eat, for the journey is too much for you." So he got up and ate and drank. Strengthened by that food, he traveled forty days and forty nights until he reached Horeb, the mountain of God. There he went into a cave and spent the night. And the word

of the LORD came to him: "What are you doing here, Elijah?" He replied, "I have been very
zealous for the LORD God Almighty. The Israelites have rejected your covenant, torn down
your altars, and put your prophets to death
with the sword. I am the only one left, and
now they are trying to kill me too." The LORD
said, "Go out and stand on the mountain in
the presence of the LORD, for the LORD is
about to pass by." Then a great and powerful
wind tore the mountains apart and shattered
the rocks before the LORD, but the LORD
was not in the wind. After the wind there was
an earthquake, but the LORD was not in the
earthquake. After the earthquake came a fire,
but the LORD was not in the fire. And after
the fire came a gentle whisper. When Elijah
heard it, he pulled his cloak over his face and
went out and stood at the mouth of the cave.
Then a voice said to him, "What are you doing
here, Elijah?"

(1 Kings 19:5–13 NIV)

God was in the whisper, not in the shout. He gave
Elijah instructions in the quiet time spent with Him,
not in the business and hustle of the day. He also gave
Elijah instructions on what to do next after his victo-

ry. God never gives us the whole story all at once. We would never finish the task because it would be too overwhelming. We obey God one day at a time, picking up our feet and doing the next thing God tells us to do. Through our obedience, there will always be healing of the soul, spirit, and body.

Healing in Obedience

> My son, attend to my words; incline your ear to my say-ings. Do not let them depart from your eyes; keep them in the midst of your heart; for they are life to those who find them, and health to all their body. Keep your heart with all diligence, for out of it are the issues of life.
>
> (Proverbs 4:20–23 MEV)

God wants us to hear Him. His words are alive and active. They are for yesterday, today, and tomorrow. God gave us the Holy Spirit to live in us so we can hear and be with Him all the time. How absolutely beautiful and full of love this is! The scripture above says to keep God's words in our hearts, for they are life and health to all of our bodies. When I am intentional and stay focused on God's Word every day, a relationship is formed. Whether I memorize scripture or not, I become familiar with

His Word. The words become who I am, and I remember what He says about me.

I've tried the other way of life without a relationship, and my life went downhill fast. I tried to fill my soul up with worldly magazines, books, movies, talk shows, and all sorts of entertainment. They never kept me content, and they never healed my heart. It was only a superficial infilling: How to lose weight, maintain shiny skin, and have beautiful hair. How to keep your spouse and friends but also have boundaries. I hoped that would be the answer to fix my lack of happiness and fit in this world. The devil wants us never to be satisfied and always to want more of this world. This world will never make us whole, healthy, and happy—only Jesus can truly bring these things to life. Jesus has so much grace, and when He sees us trying to have an intentional relationship with Him, we'll start to experience inner joy and peace. When we experience the internal pleasures of knowing Jesus, all the external things we worried about before we knew Jesus fall into place because our hearts are being healed. We don't see the external things with greed or worry as the world sees them. We see things

> *This world will never make us whole, healthy, and happy—only Jesus can truly bring these things to life.*

with God's eyes of peace and joy when we are in a relationship with Him. We choose to live differently and have more order in our lives. God likes order, not chaos, so when we walk with God, we like what He likes, and we despise what He despises. I like nice things. I like shiny cars, purses, jewelry, a nice home, order in my house, my bills paid, and good skin and hair. It's okay to like these things, but we should never put them before God. They are just pleasures that God allows us to have because He is our Father, and He wants us to enjoy the things of life.

The healing that takes place in our spirits radiates healing to our outside—our eyes, skin, and hair (our temple) radiate Jesus. Those who walk in a relationship with Jesus have a shine and a fire to them. The ones who live from the world, their shine always fades away. They may fool you for a while, but worldly living has the upper hand in their character. The fruit of living from the world are hate, unforgiveness, unhappiness, anxiety, depression, impatience, thoughtlessness, disloyalty, harshness, and impulsiveness. This is also true of us when we do not hold the truth of God in our hearts. We are underneath the problems of the world, instead of on top with victory. It reminds me of the country song by Johnny Lee that says, "I was lookin' for love in all the wrong places."[13] We are looking for healing and peace in

13 "Lookin' for Love," Johnny Lee, AZLyrics, 2022, https://www.azlyrics.com/lyrics/johnnylee/lookinforlove.html.

a world that's made up of the opposite of the goodness of God. When we live in any of the characteristics of the world, we are not living obediently to God's Word; we are living obediently to the world.

Eventually, we will become depressed, anxiety-prone, impatient, sickly, stressed out, with a bad back and an early death. God is our Healer, but the world may be our killer if we live for it. God says:

> "You shall walk in all the ways which the LORD your God has commanded you, so that you may live and that it may be well with you, and that you may prolong your days in the land which you shall possess."
>
> (Deuteronomy 5:33 MEV)

He said this so we can live, and so that it may be well for us, our children, and their children for generations. We will prosper in all the things we do, and eternal life will be ours. The commands from God come from a place of love because He is love. Also, when we give rules to our children, it's from a place of love: "Don't eat too much junk food or it will hurt your belly." "Don't touch that fire or it will burn you." "Study hard and make good grades and new doors will open for you." "Good things happen when you respect others." We teach them these things so they will prosper spiritually and maturely.

Leaning into His Word, our spirits become one with the Word. Then we are hungry to obey it. We then know what to do when the time comes to battle the things of the world, such as sadness or sickness. These things come because we are in the world. God says:

Be anxious for nothing, but in everything, by prayer and supplication with gratitude, make your requests known to God. And the peace of God, which surpasses all under-standing, will protect your hearts and minds through Christ Jesus.
(Philippians 4:6–7 MEV)

Prayer and *supplications* are words of action. When we have anxiety, we take action and pray to God. Then, in faith, we say, "Thank You for giving us peace beyond our understanding." This is praying in faith, the faith that God will uphold His promises to us. We sit still and rest in God's promise of peace and keep His Word hidden in our hearts. Even if we are not feeling peace instantly, we trust that God is manifesting peace in us. I keep a scripture above my steering wheel in my car so that when things become too much for me to handle on my own, I can read it, and God moves in my heart. Simple scriptures are good to speak into our lives throughout the day. For example:

The joy of the LORD is your strength.

(Nehemiah 8:10 MEV)

Speaking aloud God's words of amazing grace from the Bible gives me peace and strength. It's speaking and agreeing to what God is already saying in our lives.

God says His Word is *alive and active*. If something is alive and active, it is in movement. The Scriptures are moving and manifesting when you say them out loud. Speak it, believe it, and walk in it. He loves us, no matter the mistakes we make or if we're not being obedient— just like we love our obedient child just as much as our rebellious child—although the obedient one always gets to do more and has more doors open for them. It's not about one being loved more than another. It's about the obedient child learning what works and what doesn't. As God's children, we need to read His Word and find out what He desires of us. When we lean into God, He will lean in more to us. Think of it as a big, tight hug. We are letting go of taking control...*dancing with Jesus* and resting in His timing. We need to stop pulling away from His timing and trying to lead the dance. Trust and have faith that He wants to heal us.

There is a story in the Bible about Jesus encountering some lepers:

As Jesus went to Jerusalem, He passed between Samaria and Galilee. As He entered a

village, there met Him ten men who were lepers, who stood at a distance. They lifted up
their voices, saying, "Jesus, Master, have pity
on us!" When He saw them, He said to them,
"Go, show yourselves to the priests." And as
they went, they were cleansed.

(Luke17:11–14 MEV)

They heard what Jesus told them, and they were obedient. Then they were healed after they took the action
of walking. Healing can be found in our obedience and
the faith that is behind it. The evening when God healed
me inside and out, I was visiting a church. The Holy
Spirit nudged me to walk to the front, and in my obedience, God filled me with His Spirit to overflowing. He
changed my heart forever and healed me of a sciatica
nerve that had left me in pain from my neck down to the
bottom of my back. I'd had it for about thirty-five years,
and it would keep me out of work for days at a time. My
arm was beginning to go numb from the pinched nerve.
In one moment of obedience, God healed me. He healed
a wounded heart and a wounded body.

God wants to heal us physically, but more than that,
He wants to heal our hearts. I've never seen God heal a
hurt body without first touching a hurt heart. I love the
faith and obedience of the paralytic man's friends in the
Bible as they made a way to Jesus. When they lowered

their sick friend through the ceiling for Jesus to heal him, Jesus said, "You are forgiven." He not only healed the man physically, but He also healed his heart.

On a certain day, as He was teaching, Pharisees and teach-ers of the law were sitting nearby, who had come from every town of Galilee and Judea and from Jerusalem. And the power of the Lord was present to heal the sick. Now some men brought in a bed a man who was paralyzed. They searched for ways to bring him in and lay him before Him. When they could not find a way to bring him in, because of the crowd, they went up on the roof and let him down through the tiles with his bed into their midst before Jesus. When He saw their faith, He said to him, "Man, your sins are forgiven you." The scribes and the Pharisees began to question, "Who is He who speaks blasphemies? Who can forgive sins but God alone?" When Jesus per-ceived their thoughts, He answered them, "Why question in your hearts? Which is easier, to say, 'Your sins are for-given you,' or to say, 'Rise up and walk'? But that you may know that the Son of Man has authority on earth to forgive sins," He said to the paralyzed man, "I say to you,

rise, take up your bed, and go to your house."
Immediately he rose before them, and took
up that on which he lay, and departed to his
own house, glorifying God.

(Luke 5:17–25 MEV)

God did not want the man to be healed only on the
outside and not know the love of being forgiven on the
inside.

I go to the women's halfway house to teach them
about Jesus. These ladies are dealing with issues of unforgiveness and anger. They never knew how special
they are to their heavenly Father. One of the younger
ladies had a short temper and a bandage on her wrist.
She had become angry, hit the wall, and sprained it
that morning. I asked her if she wanted to see what
God would do with this. We prayed for God to heal her
wrist and waited for Holy Spirit to do what He does. He
moved through me and through her arm. He felt like fire
moving through both of us, and she began to cry. God
touched her heart and took the pain away in her wrist.
Remember, we have to take action. We spoke healing
and thanked God for manifesting the healing. She took
the bandage off her wrist and moved her wrist around,
and there was no more pain. She couldn't believe that
after she acted the way she had acted, God would still
heal her. God healed her heart and healed her wrist. He

said, You are forgiven. We should stop trying to figure God out. Take Him out of the box we have placed Him in and realize He is a God of second chances.

Letting Go of the Outcome

> LORD, my heart is not proud; my eyes are not haughty. I don't concern myself with matters too great or too awe-some for me to grasp. Instead, I have calmed and quieted myself, like a weaned child who no longer cries for its mother's milk. Yes, like a weaned child is my soul within me.
>
> (Psalm 131:1–2 NLT)

To trust the healing in our hearts and physical bodies, we have to let go of the outcome. Children trust that if their parents say something will happen, then it's going to happen. They don't concern themselves with how their parents are going to make it happen. Just like children trust in their parents, God's children trust in Him with the end results. If He doesn't want me to concern myself with how He

To trust the healing in our hearts and physical bodies, we have to let go of the outcome.

will fix something, then it's really none of my business. God is leading this dance. We just follow and rest in the security that He won't let us go. A baby cries, looking for milk from her mother. Over a period of time, she trusts that her momma is going to feed her, and she knows exactly whom to call on. Peace overcomes us when we mature in Christ and do not worry about the outcome.

Yes, we are human, and worrying about things is in our human nature. Placing our worry and cares in God's hands takes practice, as does holding His Word close to our hearts. There have been situations in my life when I've tried to lead, pull, and get the right outcome. Then God said, "Let Me lead, you follow, and I'll show you." God always has better plans than us. He'll place the desires in our hearts, but He wants us to rest in the dance. We do our part: close our eyes and allow Him to lead. His outcome will be better than our tiny plans and designs.

> For I know the plans that I have for you, says the LORD, plans for peace and not for evil, to give you a future and a hope.
> (Jeremiah 29:11 MEV)

> There are many plans in a man's heart, nevertheless the counsel of the LORD will stand.
> (Proverbs 19:21 MEV)

A man's heart devises his way, but the LORD
directs his steps.

(Proverbs 16:9 MEV)

Plans and goals are good, but God's ways are always
better and will prevail.

Losing Nick changed my outlook on life. We cannot
hang on to things, dreams, and people so tightly. Not
even our children. They are a gift from God, but they do
not truly belong to us. This is a newfound *holy fear* I have
learned. There are two different fears of an outcome.
One fear is that the situation is not how we pictured
it would be. Another is that we might lose something
special to us. These outcomes were God's first, and they
never truly belonged to us. FEAR is often referred to
as an acronym for *False Evidence Appearing Real.* I'll talk
more about fear in a later chapter, but God says there is
no fear in Christ.

There is no fear in love, but perfect love casts
out fear, be-cause fear has to do with punish-
ment. Whoever fears is not perfect in love.

(1 John 4:18 MEV)

"But seek first the kingdom of God and His
righteousness, and all these things shall be
given to you. Therefore, take no thought about

tomorrow, for tomorrow will take thought about the things of itself. Sufficient to the day is the trouble thereof."

(Matthew 6:33–34 MEV)

"Do not store up for yourselves treasures on earth where moth and rust destroy and where thieves break in and steal. But store up for yourselves treasures in heaven, where neither moth nor rust destroy and where thieves do not break in nor steal, for where your treasure is, there will your heart be also."

(Matthew 6:19–21 MEV)

We should look at everything, including our children and dreams, as gifts from God. We should not hang on so tight that we choke the life out of them. Close your eyes and place your dreams in His hands. Imagine God knitting your very own beautiful blanket of life together and creating a beautiful design. Sometimes we take the blanket back before it's finished and try to stretch it this way and that ourselves. Sometimes we hold on tight and don't allow God to knit the new patches of life on our blanket. After Mitchell finished elementary school, I used his school clothes and his baseball shirts to make a blanket. He still has many more items of clothing to wear in the future, but we've completed the elementary years so far. This has been a great beginning to his blanket of life—there are so many memories from these years and challenging work. He can look back at each shirt and see how he persevered through each sport and subject in school, how he persevered through 2019, the year when he lost his brother and won the championship with the Yard Goats baseball team.

We can do all things in Christ, who strengthens us.[14] Christ gives us supernatural strength and meets us exactly where we are. Let Him weave together each shirt you have already worn and create a beautiful design of memories. Give it back to Him and allow Him to weave a new shirt into your future blanket. We should not walk through life in fear of the future; rather, we walk with new dreams and hopes. Life doesn't usually come out as we imagine. We live long enough that we can become wounded casualties of life. But do not take your blanket back. God desires to weave new patches into the existing ones. These new patches will tie to the old patches and flow together to make the most beautiful blanket at the end of your life. In order to give our outcome to God and truly let go of the exhaustion of control, we have to forgive. Forgiveness sounds scary when we have hung on to unforgiveness for a long time. It can become our identity, but who we really are is a child of God.

---

14 See Philippians 4:13.

CHAPTER 5

Forgiveness Is a Journey

And when you stand praying, forgive if you
have anything against anyone, so that your
Father who is in heaven may also forgive you
your sins.

(Mark 11:25 MEV)

Forgiveness can be a journey and take time daily. If
you accidentally step on my toe, simply apologize and
ask for my forgiveness. I will easily forgive you and not
think about it again. But what if it's a much deeper
wound? Something that alters your life forever...a hurt
so deep, like betrayal or death. We may think the offender does not deserve our forgiveness or that we can't have
something so horrible just disappear like it never happened. If we forgive, will we be saying we are not worthy
enough in this world, and it is okay for the offender to
hurt us? What if they didn't even ask for forgiveness?

Remember, Christ was betrayed by His friends and then He was murdered. He experienced everything that we have and will. He knows our pains, and He carried all the burden for us on the cross. There is nothing we cannot forgive because Jesus already walked the path of forgiveness before us.

> *When we carry the yoke (slavery) of unforgiveness, we will become weighed down, depressed, and sick.*

For My yoke is easy, and My burden is light.
(Matthew 11:30 MEV)

In the *Holman Bible Dictionary*, a yoke is a piece of timber that is curved on each end and fitted with a shaped wooden crosspiece "to fit the necks of a pair of oxen."[15] "A chain is attached from a hook or ring in the bow and extends to the cart or load to be drawn or to the yoke of another pair of oxen behind."[16] Farmers used oxen yoked together at the time to help with fieldwork. In the Bible, a yoke means slavery or bondage, just like the Israelites were in slavery by the Egyptians. When we carry the yoke (slavery) of unforgiveness, we will become weighed down, depressed, and sick. We were not made

15 Trent C. Butler, editor, "yoke," in *Holman Bible Dictionary*, 1991, https://www.studylight.org/dictionaries/eng/hbd/y/yoke.html.
16 Ibid.

to carry unforgiveness. But with one touch from Jesus, the yoke can be lifted. When Jesus died on the cross, He took our sins on Him, one of them being unforgiveness. For us to carry unforgiveness is like saying Jesus did not do a good enough job on the cross, and we are going to take care of it ourselves.

God will not even hear our prayers if we are unforgiving. We cannot expect God to help us when we are deliberately holding on to the chains of a bitter heart of unforgiveness that keeps us weighed down in the mire of the world. If God forgave a sinner like me, I also should be able to forgive others.

> "For if you forgive other people when they sin against you, your heavenly Father will also forgive you. But if you do not forgive others their sins, your Father will not forgive your sins."
>
> (Matthew 6:14–15 NIV)

> Be kind and compassionate to one another, forgiving each other, just as in Christ God forgave you.
>
> (Ephesians 4:32 NIV)

Be angry but do not sin. Do not let the sun go
down on your anger. Do not give place to the
devil.

(Ephesians 4:26–27 MEV)

See to it that no one fails to obtain the grace
of God; that no "root of bitterness" springs up
and causes trouble, and by it many become
defiled.

(Hebrews 12:15 ESV)

Many of us walk around with unforgiveness and bitterness in our hearts. We become easily offended, and it
is difficult to maintain good relationships with others.
These types of people are easy to spot; they are usually
gossiping and thinking everything is about them. How
does a person get to be this way? We become a victim
over time, not a victor. We do not see with eternal eyes,
but with natural eyes. We can become hurt and never
release forgiveness. The devil sees an opportunity to
place a stronghold of unforgiveness on us. Then the
stronghold becomes generational and a part of our family. It is stuck and ingrained in us for generations. This
is how the devil works. We can ask God to remove this
stronghold from us, and He will. We can be the fore-
runner for our family to break the generational curse of
unforgiveness. He can give us the tools we need to walk
in freedom.

The Devil Does Not Want Us to Forgive Ourselves

We know that all things work together for good to those who love God, to those who are the called according to His purpose. For whom He foreknew, He also predestined to be conformed to the image of His Son, that He might be the firstborn among many brethren. Moreover whom He predestined, these He also called; whom He called, these He also justified; and whom He justified, these He also glorified.

(Romans 8:28–30 NKJV)

Peter felt so much shame after denying Jesus that he went back to what he knew before Jesus. He went back to fishing. When we are ashamed and cannot forgive ourselves, we tend to go back to what we knew before the freedom of Jesus. Drinking, drugs, unforgiveness, or hiding from people are all ways we deal with shame. Fishing obviously does not make us a victim of shame, but using it as a

> *When we are ashamed and cannot forgive ourselves, we tend to go back to what we knew before the freedom of Jesus.*

crutch to hide from God does. At the beginning of Peter's testimony, Jesus walked by him and said, "Follow
me, and I will make you fishers of men!"[17] They became
great friends, but when Peter told Jesus he would die
for Him, Jesus said, "No, Peter, you will deny Me three
times before the rooster crows."[18]

Peter felt so much shame because he did eventually
do just that. After the cross, Jesus wanted to reinstate
Peter. Jesus cooked breakfast on the beach that morning. Peter saw Him from his boat and ran to Him.

> So when they had eaten breakfast, Jesus said
> to Simon Pe-ter, "Simon, son of John, do you
> love Me more than these?" He said to Him,
> "Yes, Lord. You know that I love You." He
> said to him, "Feed My lambs." He said to him
> again a second time, "Simon, son of John, do
> you love Me?" He said to Him, "Yes, Lord. You
> know that I love You." He said to him, "Tend
> My sheep." He said to him the third time, "Si-
> mon, son of John, do you love Me?" Pe-ter was
> grieved because He asked him the third time,
> "Do you love Me?" He said to Him, "Lord, You
> know every-thing. You know that I love You."
> Jesus said to him, "Feed My sheep."
>
> (John 21:15–17 MEV)

---

17 Matthew 4:19.
18 See Matthew 26:34.

We are all human, and we are going to make mistakes. Some mistakes will be bigger than others, but God does not want us to hang on to any of them. He says we are conformed to the image of His Son because of the cross. We are justified and glorified because we carry Jesus within us. The devil does not, under any circumstances, want us to be free. He condemns us, whispers in our ears of our guilt, and tells us we are not worthy and that we should never forgive ourselves for what we did. He tells us we should wear unforgiveness like a badge. We will know the difference between the devil's actions and Jesus' actions by the fruit of what we experience. Jesus convicts, but the devil will condemn. When we are convicted by the Holy Spirit, our sin is brought to our hearts. Then we know this is something we need to work on and give to Jesus to help us through. When we are feeling condemnation, we want to hide like Peter did. We feel we are not worthy enough ever to be forgiven, and we judge ourselves against an unattainable standard with none of the grace of God. This is how we end up becoming a martyr, a victim, and not a victor.

The definition of *condemnation* is "penalty, an adverse sentence,"[19] but the definition of convict is "to expose, rebuke, refute, reprove, show fault."[20] Peter was allow-

---

19 James Strong, "Condemnation," In *Strong's Exhaustive Concordance of the Bible* (New York: Abingdon Press, 1890a).
20 James Strong, "Convict," In *Strong's Exhaustive Concordance of the Bible* (New York: Abingdon Press, 1890b).

ing his conviction to turn into condemnation on himself. Jesus gave Peter the opportunity to forgive himself, to tell Jesus he loved Him as many times as he had denied Him. Jesus needed Peter to forgive himself so he could do Kingdom work and fish for men again. He removed the condemnation of the devil from Peter.

Jesus does not want us to carry unforgiveness within ourselves. We are looking with the natural eyes, but we need to look with the eyes of the eternal Kingdom of God. We cannot work for the Kingdom of God if we carry condemnation on ourselves. We have to understand that this world is temporary and that all things can be forgiven. With condemnation, we will not think we are good enough.

> There is therefore now no condemnation for those who are in Christ Jesus, who walk not according to the flesh, but according to the Spirit.
>
> (Romans 8:1 MEV)

God loves us so much that He gave us a way out. He already knew you would do that thing you did. He does not approve of the sin, but He also doesn't want us to carry unforgiveness of ourselves. He is the only One who is able to remove the guilt and unforgiveness. He tells us to release it to Him, and He will do the rest. Yes, there is

> *God loves us so much He gave us a way out. He already knew you would do that thing you did.*

work on our part, but we can rest in the assurance that He will do His part.

To release unforgiveness to God, we start with a prayer.

Heavenly Father, help me to forgive myself. This burden is too heavy for me to carry. I know You knew I would do this. I also know You want to help me out of this hole I have dug myself in. I repent for the things I have done. I am sorry for holding on to these things, and I release them to You. I ask You to free me and fill me with the Holy Spirit so that I can be directed and filled with wisdom and knowledge from You. I love You, and I thank You in advance for what You are doing and will do.

Sometimes, with healing, we have to release things to God daily. When we feel the condemnation trying to come back on us, we tell the devil to go away. God says there is no condemnation in Christ for His children, and that is us. This might have to be a daily *let go and let God* prayer or an every-ten-minutes prayer. When we continue to do this, we will start to feel the lifting of the heaviness. But remember, God doesn't need to hear this over and over. What we feel and what is truth are two different things. Repeating it is really just for us until we receive an eternal mindset. We walk in the truth and allow Jesus to do the rest, and He will.

When we mess up God's power is there to see us through. He has a destiny for us to fulfill, a purpose, and a plan for our lives.[21]

Forgiveness Is an Action

Then Peter came to Him and said, "Lord, how often shall my brother sin against me, and I forgive him? Up to seven times?" Jesus said to him, "I do not say to you, up to sev-en times, but up to seventy times seven."

(Matthew 18:21–22 NKJV)

This was not my favorite scripture. We have to walk in a forgiving heart. This is a challenging thing to do. But God is the answer. We have to walk in a repentant heart. Only Jesus can help us with this. I never understood why I would need to forgive someone who was in the wrong. Just let them go their way, and I will go mine—that was my philosophy. The thing about that

---

21 Kenneth Hagin, *Following God's Plan For Your Life*. Electronic. Faith Library Publications, 2011.

mindset is that I was holding unforgiveness in my heart and cutting myself off from the sunlight of the Spirit. Any grudges, unforgiveness, or offenses cut us off from God. God didn't say you had to be best friends with the person who offended you, but He said you have to forgive them and release them to Him, so He can take care of the situation.

Knowing that God will take care of the situation is enough for me to let go and forgive. We might not feel relief at first when we say we forgive the other person. This also might be something that we can only say to God. Forgiveness is an action on our part. The hard part of forgiving is to say it. The easy part is to let go and allow God to do His thing.

> *We do not rely on our feelings but on God's truth. His truth trumps our feelings.*

We do not rely on our feelings but on God's truth. His truth trumps our feelings. Feelings do change, but God's Word stands through eternity. Others have intentionally hurt my family and me. God showed me how to see these offenses with eternal eyes. We are here only for a short while on this earth. Some people's journeys will be shorter than others. God wants us to be filled to the brim with His presence for all our days. He wants us to carry a freedom that we can only get from Him.

We can read all the self-help books and go to all the therapy sessions we want, but when we release a person who has done us wrong into God's care, then we take action to unyoke ourselves from unforgiveness. We allow God to fill us with Him. Think about this. Our loved ones are free and unyoked and cheering us on in heaven. They know we will all be together again, and they know we need freedom as they have. We have siblings in Christ in heaven and on earth.

> For this reason I bow my knees to the Father of
> our Lord Jesus Christ, from whom the whole
> family in heaven and earth is named,
> (Ephesians 3:14–15 MEV)

Our goal is to be free, like our heavenly brothers and sisters. In his book *The Great Divorce*, C.S. Lewis describes hell as a place where no one forgets anything; they remember every cruel word and every wrong that was ever done to them.[22] They are completely unforgiving. In heaven, all things are new and put away. We want a heavenly mindset, not one that is rooted in hell.

When we carry unforgiveness, it shows on our faces and bodies. With unforgiveness, we have stress. This leads to illnesses. We can have diseases, cancers, bad backs, and age quickly. This is not what God wants for

---

22 C.S. Lewis, *The Great Divorce* (HarperCollins, 1945, 2002).

us. I am not saying these things always stem from unforgiveness, but I have seen miracles of healing take place when people forgive. I knew a lady who for years always was talking about people in a hateful manner. She had unforgiveness in her heart, and it grew worse every time I saw her. She was full of bitterness and made herself a victim in everything she said. She came and saw me one day and said she had breast cancer. I spoke to her about letting the bitterness go; she never would, and she never got better. It's not the cause of every case of cancer for sure, but unforgiveness and bitterness can manifest themselves in many sicknesses. God says to forgive; it's a command. To be whole and complete, we need to walk in a repentant, forgiving stance. We are not doormats, letting others treat us poorly with no repercussions, but we do allow God to show us how to deal with each situation. In time, we learn to move and dance with Jesus. Let Him lead because He is the only way.

If you're holding on to unforgiveness, there will be something like a wall over you when you pray. God will not hear you.

> But your iniquities have separated you from your God; your sins have hidden his face from you...
>
> (Isaiah 59:2 NIV)

One evening, I was praying for a lady who was not receiving what Jesus wanted to give her. I felt a complete wall around her. The prayer was not going anywhere, and it was completely of her making, not God's. God told me she carried unforgiveness, so I asked her whom she needed to forgive. Finally, after some nudging, she confessed she needed to forgive her mother. I said, "Repeat after me," and I led her through a prayer, and she forgave. She took action, and as soon as she forgave, she was set free. The devil had to let her go, and the unforgiving spirit left her. She allowed God's light to shine in her spirit. God touched her, and she crumpled to the floor. He filled her with the peace and joy of the Holy Spirit.

To learn to forgive, say the following prayer with me. We might have to pray this daily until we feel released. Remember, God only needs this once; the other times are just for you. Truth trumps feelings. To the person who hurt us, we say, "I forgive you."

Heavenly Father, I forgive _____. I lay them at the altar before You. I am sorry I carried this unforgiveness. I know they have done me wrong, but I also know You can take better care of this than I can. I cannot carry this heaviness anymore. I release them fully to You and pray that You bless them. Fill me with Your peace and the joy of the

Holy Spirit. Direct my steps from here on out. Create in me a new heart and allow me to see with Your eyes. Thank You, Jesus, for taking all of my sins on the cross. This I pray in Jesus' name.

There is fear behind all things not of God, including unfor-giveness. In the next chapter, we will find out how to release that fear and dance more in step with Jesus.

CHAPTER 6

But God, I'm Scared

And He said to him, "Truly, truly I say to you, hereafter you shall see heaven opened and the angels of God as-cending and descending upon the Son of Man."

(John 1:51 MEV)

I was driving to the cemetery one morning to visit Nicholas's grave when I felt an uncontrollable wave of emotion coming on. It was a wave of anxiety and fear trying to envelop me. I said, "God, I'm really scared right now, and my heart hurts so bad it feels like it could break in half. I need to know what Nick is doing right now." The song "I Can Only Imagine" came on the radio instantly. That was the last song that was played at his funeral. I started laughing with tears in my eyes like only someone who knows Jesus can do. Soon I was sitting next to Nicholas's grave on a bench, as I begged God to let me see an angel.

When I am in that state of sadness, I find so much comfort in the fact that only a veil separates us from heaven. One morning, as I was sitting in that exact spot, there was a tiny red bird in the tree, all by himself, next to me. He was just sitting on the branch looking at me. Later on, as I was driving back home from the gravesite, I was stopped at a red light. While waiting for the red light, I saw a beautiful white feather as it floated down, right in front of my car. It was the most amazing thing. I looked up, there were no trees around, and it was a busy road. But the feather floated right down in front of my car—it was a gift for me from God. He loves us so much, and when we ask, He delivers. He placed me back in the moment of reality, to see how close heaven and earth are connected. I asked to see an angel, and He delivered.

> *He placed me back in the moment of reality, of how close heaven and earth are connected.*

In the story of Jacob and Esau, Jacob was in fear because he had deceived his brother, and he had then run for his life, never to see any of his family again, or so he thought. He laid his head on a rock, fell asleep, and had a dream from God.

When he reached a certain place, he stopped
for the night because the sun had set. Taking
one of the stones there, he put it under his
head and lay down to sleep. He had a dream in
which he saw a stairway resting on the earth,
with its top reaching to heaven, and the angels of God were as-cending and descending
on it. There above it stood the LORD, and he
said: "I am the LORD, the God of your father
Abraham and the God of Isaac. I will give you
and your descendants the land on which you
are lying. Your descendants will be like the
dust of the earth, and you will spread out to
the west and to the east, to the north and to
the south. All peoples on earth will be blessed
through you and your offspring. I am with
you and will watch over you wherever you go,
and I will bring you back to this land. I will
not leave you until I have done what I have
promised you."

(Genesis 28:11–15 NIV)

The angels of God were ascending and descending
on the ladder that reached to heaven. Jacob realized
there was an open heaven, and he could have contact
with the angels. If we have direct access to heaven, what
can we really fear? God is with us even in our scariest

times. The worst thing that can happen is death. Then, only our flesh dies, not our spirits, and God takes us up the ladder to heaven. Jesus is the ladder to heaven (John 1:51). God told Jacob that He was with him and would protect him. God would not leave him until what was promised to Jacob came forth. So, in the waiting, we remember that God will not forsake us, and His promises will come forth.

> *In the waiting, we remember that God will not forsake us, and His promises will come forth.*

We can have peace in the fact that heaven is not far away. I imagine the veil from here to heaven is so thin that birds can even fly through it. If angels can descend on a ladder from heaven to earth, why can't God send a redbird from heaven to earth? When I see the eternal of this world, it becomes less scary and more beautiful.

The Secret behind Fear

> He rose and rebuked the wind, and said to the sea, "Peace, be still!" Then the wind ceased and there was a great calm.
>
> (Mark 4:39 MEV)

Jesus was sleeping through the thunderstorm on the boat. The disciples woke Him because they were in fear. That's when He called for peace.

> He said to them, "Why are you so fearful? How is that you have no faith?"
>
> (Mark 4:40 MEV)

Fear is a powerful word. There is a healthy fear and an unhealthy fear. A healthy fear is not placing your hand in a snake pit because you know you will get bit. It's not jumping out of an airplane without a parachute. Healthy fears are commonsense fears that God has ingrained within us. An unhealthy fear, on the other hand, is learned behavior, and it is not from God; it is from the devil. Fear is behind worry, pride, greed, lust, anger, gluttony, envy, and sloth. Anytime we are acting in any of these ways, fear is the driving force behind it.

Unhealthy fear is not "in the now." It is in the future and in the past. When I am hit with a wave of fear or anxiety, I have to talk to myself to calm down. I name where my family members are at that exact moment. After losing Nick, I was afraid of everything being out of control. It would hit me so hard I could not breathe. Doctors called it post-traumatic stress disorder. So I would start naming where people were in the now. I would say, "Mitch is at school, Zack is at work, Bill is at home, and Nick is in heaven right at this moment." Yes, Nick is in heaven, and I cannot physically be with him, but I can know at that exact moment he is safe. Everything at this exact moment is okay. The fear and anxiety I held was in the guilt of the past, which the devil would try to use against me. The fear was also in the future of not being able to see Nick or something happening to my other children. It's a hard place to live—in the future or the past—because there can be no peace. There is only peace in the now. The next time you are in fear, remember that the veil is thin and God is here, and then get back in the moment.

There is the fear of losing something or someone we had or never had. There is the fear of being fearful—what a horrible way to make it through a day! We have become victims and allowed the devil to speak lies to our hearts. To have complete freedom, we have to be fearless. How do we become fearless? We recognize when we are in fear. When we do not recognize where our emotions come from, we are out of control. Here is an example. Abraham's wife, Sarah, was promised a baby in the Bible.

> *There is the fear of losing something or someone we had or never had.*

Then God said to Abraham, "As for Sarai your wife, you will not call her name Sarai, but her name will be Sarah. I will bless her and also give you a son by her. I will bless her, and she will be the mother of nations. Kings of peoples will come from her."

(Genesis 17:15–16 MEV)

She waited and watched other women have babies. She was growing old, worried, and jealous. But God's ways are not our ways. He always does things in His time, especially if it is fulfilling His promises for His glory. Because Sarah did not wait for God's timing and she gave another woman to her husband to have a baby, there were bitter roots. Generationally, we are still affected today.

She gave another woman to her husband to fulfill the promise to herself. Remember, God told Jacob:

"I will not leave you until I have done what I have prom-ised you."

(Genesis 28:15 NIV)

His promises were for Sarah and also for us.

For all the promises of God in Him are "Yes,"
and in Him "Amen," to the glory of God
through us.

(2 Corinthians 1:20 MEV)

Twenty-five years later, Sarah had her baby, and God's promise was fulfilled. Sarah was in fear of losing something she did not have yet. She was in fear of the future. She was not trusting and resting on the promise. If Sarah had brought herself back into the present, it would have been easier to rest in God's promise. The fear she felt caused worry, jealousy, and anger. God's anointing and peace for Sarah were in her now, and she was right where she was supposed to be at the moment. She did not have healthy tools to recognize that her fears were not from God. We need to learn our emotions, trust the process, and keep letting Jesus lead the dance. The blessings are in the "now." The most important part of our prayer is the faith and fifteen minutes after our prayer. Trust that God heard your prayer and lean in that He is behind the scenes making it happen. Remember, we live by faith, not by sight.

For we live by faith, not by sight.

(2 Corinthians 5:7 NIV)

The Fear of Success

> But you are a chosen race, a royal priesthood,
> a holy na-tion, a people for God's own posses-
> sion, so that you may declare the goodness of
> Him who has called you out of darkness into
> His marvelous light.
>
> (1 Peter 2:9 MEV)

God called us out of the ordinary to be lights to a dark
world. We are God's children and called to stand out.
God has our backs, and He wants us to succeed more
than we do. So why do we get comfortable and give up
on our God-given dreams? Because we are afraid of
success or the demanding work, and we self-sabotage
ourselves. We get in the way of our dreams because we
are in fear that we are not good enough. We don't realize we have been chosen for such a time as this, to be
called out, and we forget the dream came from God. Peo-

People who self-sabotage rarely look at their part in a failed situation, only somebody else's part.

ple who self-sabotage rarely look at their part in a failed
situation, only somebody else's part. Then it becomes
a created mountain that's not true in their minds, that

is too big for them to conquer, and they give up. God wants us to tell that mountain to move!

> For truly I say to you, whoever says to this mountain, "Be removed and be thrown into the sea," and does not doubt in his heart, but believes that what he says will come to pass, he will have whatever he says.
>
> (Mark 11:23 MEV)

The fear of other people is one of the reasons we self-sabotage. We can give negative talk to ourselves all day when we do not know to whom we belong. I was driving my son to school one day, and we were talking about his schoolwork. I said to Mitch, "God called you to stand out, not to be mediocre. We are the King's children, and that makes you a prince." The negative self-talk comes from the devil, but the positive talk comes from God. The devil wants you to second-guess who you are and how special you are. The dream burns stronger in our hearts and doesn't fade away easily. It is up to us how we nurture the dream and follow the lead of Jesus. He will lead us through our dreams, step by step, when we learn to follow His moves. The devil will try his best to throw kinks in our plan, and he hopes we will give up. When God placed this book in my spirit, I had no idea how to go about writing a book. I could have listened with my natural ears and not trusted the push from God.

The devil whispered, *Who do you think you are? You never even finished high school, and you are just a hairdresser.* I said back to him, "Yes, that is true, but I love Jesus, I study the Word, I've led many Bible classes, I have been ordained in ministry, I have been to different countries serving Jesus, and I have seen many miracles. I have shared Jesus in the prisons and halfway houses, and I have experienced a loss beyond comprehension. I'm not just a hairdresser. I love people. I have established relationships for twenty-seven years, and I'm full of wisdom and knowledge from God. But even if I didn't do any of these things, I am still God's daughter. I am a princess in His Kingdom, and I cannot be any more loved by God than I am right now." He leads me, and I follow. If a direction pivots, then I pivot with it, and I follow the glory of God. If we follow His glory, then there is no fear because He always makes it happen.

> *If a direction pivots, then I pivot with it, and I follow the glory of God.*

God spoke to my heart that there would be healing in this book for others and for me. He showed me how to outline and organize. Then I was introduced to an editor and a publisher. Everything about this book has been God-ordained. God created everybody, and we all have fears. But what separates the adults from the children

A L L I S O N   B R O U G H T O N

is how we manage those fears. We are either a victim or a victor; we get to choose. Eleanor Roosevelt once said:

> You gain strength, courage and confidence by every expe-rience in which you really stop to look fear in the face. You are able to say to yourself, "I have lived through this horror. I can take the next thing that comes along." You must do the thing you think you cannot do.[23]

---

23 "Quote by Eleanor Roosevelt," BrainyQuote, 2022, https://www.brainyquote.com/quotes/eleanor_roosevelt_121157.

CHAPTER 7

Eternally Free

"Let the beloved of the LORD rest secure
in him, for he shields him all day long, and
the one the LORD loves rests between his
shoulders."

(Deuteronomy 33:12 NIV)

God gave me a beautiful movie vision one afternoon.
I was in a beautiful dark green forest. The morning light
was trying to shine through, but the trees were full and
tall, blocking the sun. As I was standing in the forest, I
looked down, and lying on the ground beside me was
my body, lifeless. I then looked at myself standing there,
and I was wearing warrior-fitted gold clothes, holding a
cool sword and a key. Then I took off running and came
to a door that opened with my key. When I walked in,
there were gold, shiny treasures everywhere. God said,
"Whatever you ask for, I will give you." I said, "God, You
know I do not care about treasures. I just want Nicho-

las back." God replied, "You cannot have him; he is with Me." I knew this, but my heart still ached for him.

Then I looked across the room and saw a gold treasure box. I went to it and pulled out gifts from God: a diploma, a baton, a dip ink pen, and a crown. These all have special meaning to me. God said, "I'm giving you a supernatural diploma." I did not graduate from high school. Instead, I took a test and received my GED when I was eighteen, and He knew this had always bothered me. I did graduate with a Bible school diploma from Rhema Correspondence Bible School, which I had worked on for two years, and I was ordained in ministry right after this vision. When God gives you a baton, it does not matter what anybody does. It cannot be taken away. A baton is a mantle handed down; it is a spiritual inheritance from God. My baton is a sum of all the lessons, insights, counsel, character, and spiritual anointing I have received from God in my lifetime. The dip ink pen is because of the book I'm writing. He said it would be supernatural and anointed, and that it will help many. The crown, of course, demonstrates that I am God's child. God showed me that all the treasures He has for me are mine, but I had to ask and receive.

Imagine all the treasures in heaven we do not receive because we do not ask.

Imagine all the treasures in heaven we do not receive because we do not ask.

The important thing about this vision was that I did not have to strive for anything. He knew the desires of my heart, and He handed them to me. I have done my part of what He has asked in obedience (I say yes), and I allowed God to do His. God tells us to rest in Him and all of our heart's desires will come forth. God places me where He wants me. He has people invite me to events, so I don't have to invite myself. He stirs things up in my heart, and because I rest in Him, I hear Him. He tells me to go pray with a young lady sitting by herself, and I do. This is truly eternal-minded rest. Everything is for God's heavenly Kingdom, and we want what is done in heaven to be done here on earth.

> "Our Father who is in heaven, hallowed be Your name. Your kingdom come; Your will be done on earth, as it is in heaven."
> (Matthew 6:9–10 MEV)

There is a purpose in resting in God because we can hear Him better. When we hear Him better, our work becomes more in line with His Kingdom.

We might be excelling at the tasks under which we labor, but they might not be what God is telling us to do. Of course, anything we do that is good is Kingdom work. We might not even realize the thing He created us distinctly for because we never rested in His presence long enough to hear Him. I could not have written this book without God's knowledge and wisdom. I never stressed over it, but I rested in it. He showed me how to do it step by step and word for word. When I say "rest," I do not mean sleep, but resting in Jesus' presence during the day. When we can rest in Him, our sleep at night and our productivity during the day are better.

I was cleaning the bathroom at my house one day when I said, "I praise You, Jesus, that I have a beautiful house and a toilet to clean." When I was a teenager, I would drive by the neighborhood I live in now and think I would never get to live there. It wasn't that I wanted to; it was just a passing thought. I did not understand the grace and love of Jesus. So as I cleaned the bathroom in my house, I said, "Thank You, Jesus, because You know my heart's desires even before I do."

In the vision I mentioned earlier, when I left my old body on the ground in the forest, God said, "I have made you anew, and you will leave your old body and take up your new."

> That you put off the former way of life in the old nature, which is corrupt according to the deceitful lusts, and be re-newed in the spirit of your mind; and that you put on the new na-

ture, which was created according to God in
right-eousness and true holiness.

(Ephesians 4:22–24 MEV)

My old person strived to do it on her own, but she
wore herself out. My new person, with the renewed
mind and body, could go to work outside of the home,
clean house, cook supper, help Mitchell with homework,
write this book, exercise, be with friends and family,
and do so much more, all in rest.

A few meanings of rest from *Merriam-Webster* are
"peace of mind and spirit; place for resting and lodg-
ing; free from anxiety or disturbance; and refrain from
labor or exertion."[24] We can find all these definitions of
rest in Jesus. The only way to have rest in our day and
night is to ask God to empty us of the sins holding us
back.

Where Jesus removes the sins that are holding us in
bondage, He will replace them with peace and love of
Himself. He promised us this.

But the Advocate, the Holy Spirit, whom the
Father will send in my name, will teach you
all things and will remind you of everything
I have said to you. Peace I leave with you; my

---

24 "Rest," in *Merriam-Webster Online Dictionary*. Merriam-Webster, Incorporated,
2022, https://www.merriam-webster.com/dictionary/rest.

peace I give you. I do not give to you as the world gives. Do not let your hearts be troubled and do not be afraid.

(John 14:26–27 NIV)

> *If we are busy striving all the time, then we cannot hear God to follow His heart.*

My old self strived and competed in everything. Behind the striving and competing were the sins of worry and the fear of not being good enough. Look at the fault behind anything that does not line up with God and repent of it. God says that I am the apple of His eye.

Keep me as the apple of Your eye; hide me under the shadow of Your wings.

(Psalm 17:8 MEV)

Why do I need to strive when He loves to lead me? I just follow the glory cloud of His Presence, and He leads me where I need to go.

And He said, "My Presence will go with you, and I will give you rest." Then he said to Him,

"If Your Presence does not go with us, do not
bring us up from here."
(Exodus 33:14–15 MEV)

Moses was speaking to God, and he did not want to
go anywhere without Him. Moses was leading the Israelites to freedom from slavery in the Old Testament,
and they followed God's presence through the desert.
They followed His presence in a cloud by day and fire
by night so they would not get lost, and they always had
His peace and protection with them. Because of Jesus,
we now have the Holy Spirit, whom we get to carry with
us at all times. If we are busy laboring all the time, then
we cannot hear God and follow His heart. The Israelites
chose not to follow God toward the end of the journey to
what could have been their Promised Land. They grum-
bled and complained all the time and so they walked in
circles for forty years. They never made it to the Promised Land because they did not fully trust God, but their
children did because God has grace and mercy. If they
had stayed close to His presence and trusted Him, it
might have just taken a few days to get to the Promised
Land. Let us choose to follow God's presence and stay in
His rest. Miracles happen in God's rest—like the restoration of relationships.

Resting in Restoration

Do not remember the former things nor con-
sider the things of old. See, I will do a new
thing, now it shall spring forth; shall you not
be aware of it? I will even make a way in the
wilderness, and rivers in the desert.

(Isaiah 43:18–19 MEV)

One day Nicholas was going through various pains
and struggles, and he did not agree with the way I was
doing things. He became deeply angry at me. I'm not exactly sure what happened, and I cannot speak for him,
but he would not talk to me. Days turned into months,
and then months turned into two years. It is easier to
be mad at the person who loves you; you know they will
not turn against you. When Nicholas was born, I was
young and not married, and I did not tell him who his
biological father was until he was much older. It was a
bad choice on my part; I should have been honest from
the beginning, but I cannot go back and change it now.
We just do the best we can with what we have, and that
was all I had in my twenties. I was in survival mode and
was not walking with Jesus yet.

Nicholas loved me very much, but he was angry
about this situation, and I was easily to blame for everything else going wrong. His heart was big. He would

drop what he was doing to help anybody, but he was also twenty-three and struggling with battles of his own. I had faith that God would walk him through them, as God did with me when I had battles in my younger years. I would call and text him once a week throughout this time and say, "I love you"; I did that for two years. I invited him over to visit and eat. I would send scriptures to him, or whatever was on my heart, and never receive a call or a text back. I just kept moving in faith, but my heart grieved and hurt so bad. I just rested and trusted that God would make my family right again. I have seen miracles follow Nicholas, and I knew God was not done with him yet. One day, I went to lunch, and when I came back, he was standing there, waiting for me. This was the beginning of a new relationship between us.

I treaded carefully and allowed God to take the wheel. "The biblical meaning of the word 'restoration' is to receive back more than has been lost to the point where the final state is greater than the original condition. The main point is that someone or something is improved beyond measure."[25] Nicholas needed that time away from me to grow, and he was more spiritually mature than he was before. As a result, our relationship was stronger, and I could count on him to be there when he said he would. God placed it on my heart to start cooking supper with the boys and grandkids once

25 "Rest," in *Merriam-Webster Online Dictionary*, 2022.

a month. That way, I could have them all at the house at the same time. I was very intentional about it, and we all enjoyed each other. When we rest in God's presence, we can hear Him stirring up ideas in our hearts. I did not know He was preparing us for when He would take Nicholas home to heaven. Nicholas wanted to come and hang out at the beach house with us more often, and I was able to spend quality time with him and take great photos of the boys at the beach. These were all big events happening in our family. He was running toward us and not from us.

God restored our family beyond measure. This was an answer to the prayers I had prayed as I walked the floor with my grandmother's Bible for years and prayed scriptures. I was on my knees in faith all hours of the night for Nicholas. For years, I had wanted a family picture, but I could not get my family together to get one. Mitchell had a big school event, and both Nicholas and Zachary came to support their brother. This is so important; God was really blessing us. Then we went out to eat at Buffalo Wild Wings, and we were all were standing together, and my friend said, "Turn around, I want to take your picture." We were all together, and we made funny faces and smiles for our unplanned family picture. None of us could have planned that, but God is faithful, and He gave us grace and this opportunity for a fun family picture. He is sovereign and knew all the days of Nicholas. Five days later, Nicholas was gone from this earth and in God's house, as my granddaughter says. He is in our future now. Every day is a day closer to seeing him again. His days were numbered, and God wanted Nick in heaven more than on earth. He gave us more heart-healing before so we could have closure here on earth. I thank God for the restoration and mercy He showed us, even though I will miss Nicholas every day until I see him again.

We would never have had that special time together if both of us were not walking and resting in what God was telling us to do. We had to let go of the past and allow God to make us new. Jesus is in the restoration business, and He restores our hearts, minds, and spirits. He has restored many of our relationships since Nicholas passed. We shouldn't walk

> *Jesus is in the restoration business, and He restores our hearts, minds, and spirits.*

this earth in bitterness and always hold on to the past. God was there in our past, in our now, and in our future. God has shown me that heaven is amazing, and that this earth is just a taste of what heaven will be like. He has allowed me to see Nicholas with horses, with children, climbing mountains with a backpack, and with friends his own age in heaven. I have seen him instructing children and working at his job. He had a pencil behind his ear and a lot of papers in front of him. Then he was walking fast through a city to give the papers to somebody. Heaven is busy and wonderful, and things are moving fast there. I felt in my heart that they are getting busy for all of us.

Don't be bothered by the things holding you down on this earth. We are spirits with flesh around our spirits, made for walking and breathing on this earth. God created each of us, and He knows every hair on our heads. He didn't misplace Nicholas or any of us. He knows exactly where all His children are, in heaven and on earth. When we receive Jesus, our spirit becomes a re-created spirit intertwined with Jesus' Spirit. If we shake off worldly things, we can accept healing in our relationships and healing in our flesh. Our spirit is stronger than our flesh. When we are weighted down in this world, our spirits become sickly, and so does our flesh. People who stay close to Jesus have a shine about them in their eyes and their skin. The eyes are the window to our spirits and souls, so when we rest in Jesus' healing, our spirits, and our physical bodies, fall into place.

Resting in Healing

But he was wounded for our transgressions,
he was bruised for our iniquities; the chas-

tisement of our peace was upon him, and by his stripes we are healed.

(Isaiah 53:5 MEV)

It's not how many prayers we pray or the way we pray them that allows us to receive healing in our bodies. It is faith in our Creator that He has already healed us on the cross. When Jesus was on the cross, He defeated the devil. Jesus took the penalty for our sins so we could have forgiveness and peace. He was beaten and nailed to the cross for our disobedience. When I make bad choices—and I know better and still do the wrong thing—the Holy Spirit convicts me. I'm able to repent and ask for forgiveness because of Jesus' wounds. I am already forgiven because the sacrifice has already been made. The closer we walk with Jesus, the fewer bad choices we actually decide to make.

> *When we sin against somebody we love, we ask forgiveness out of love for them and the love of Christ.*

I am justified and sanctified because of Jesus, and I am His child. When we are God's children, He wants us to be aware of our sins so we can ask Him to forgive us and walk in freedom from them. When we sin against somebody we love, we ask for forgiveness out of love for them and the love of Christ.

Servants, respectfully obey your earthly mas-
ters but al-ways with an eye to obeying the
real master, Christ. Don't just do what you
have to do to get by, but work heartily, as
Christ's servants doing what God wants you
to do. And work with a smile on your face,
always keeping in mind that no matter who
happens to be giving the orders, you're really
serving God. Good work will get you good pay
from the Master, regardless of whether you
are slave or free.

(Ephesians 6:5–8 MSG)

If we are Christians and we use the grace card for
everything and walk in sin continuously, there will be
consequences. Yes, we are forgiven because of the cross,
but He is a God of justice. There will be a day of judgment one day, and it will affect our rewards in heaven.
When we are walking in a close relationship with God
and we have the love of Christ, we want to do the right
thing by God no matter the heavenly reward because we
are changed spirit beings. To receive our healing, we
need to be walking in Jesus' freedom and love of others.

When they whipped Jesus and made stripes on His
back, He took on our sicknesses inside and out. Scripture says, "...by his stripes we are healed"—not *will* be

healed, but *are* healed.[26] We often receive our salvation and stop there, and yes, that is enough, but what Jesus did for us on the cross was so much more. He gave us eternal life and also took on our sickness! To receive Jesus' salvation, we have to speak and receive Him in faith. To receive Jesus' healing, we have to speak and receive His healing in faith. Jesus already did all the horrible, bloody work for us. We do not have to strive for salvation, and we do not have to strive for our healing. We receive both in a restful state because we are spiritual beings with flesh around us.

> I say then, walk in the Spirit, and you shall not fulfill the lust of the flesh. For the flesh lusts against the Spirit, and the Spirit against the flesh. These are in opposition to one another, so that you may not do the things that you please.
>
> (Galatians 5:16–17 MEV)

Our flesh is in constant war with our spirits, so we have to learn to rest our spirits in the way God chooses to heal us.

Thank Him for healing your spirit and your body, and stay in faith that it has happened already. In God's eyes, it is already done, so we need to simply wait for

---

26 Isaiah 53:5b.

our flesh to catch up with what our spirits already know. The most important part of our prayer is what we believe and say fifteen minutes after it. Our prayer can be canceled out by what we say, so keep thanking God for His healing. We can receive God's report or the devil's report; it's up to us. The devil says you will never get better, so you might as well give up. God says to trust Him; His yoke is not heavy. Let go of striving and just dance in His steps. We have authority over our flesh because we carry Jesus' authority. We walk in authority and rest in the way God is healing us. It could be in an instant, in a couple of weeks, through a doctor, or it could be in heaven, which is where we will receive our complete healing. But we must walk in faith that we are healed already and receive how it will be manifested. Remember, God is not of time; He is in the past, present, and future all at once. We cannot put a time limit on Him.

I have been healed instantly of fever and other ailments because I commanded the sickness to leave, and I have also had a painful elbow for weeks. Now, this elbow is from work and continuous movement that I have done for twenty-seven years. I choose to believe there will be total healing someday, but in my waiting and resting, I have used creams and taken anti-inflammatories. I do not believe Jesus wants me to stay in pain until my healing is manifested. I will rest pain-free with what the doctors suggest until it is completely healed by God. We reach for Jesus' hem first. That is *dancing with Jesus* and letting go of the limiting thoughts that He heals only a certain way. Trust His process and take Him out of the box in which you may have placed Him.

For healing, pray this prayer in faith and rest in faith that He will do it:

> *Father, I praise You for You are my Healer, and I thank You for the cross. By Your stripes I am healed of_____. I command the pain to leave with the authority of Christ I carry. I trust how You will manifest my healing, and I will rest with peace that You are my Healer. I thank you for healing _____. Amen.*

Now, do something with the faith that you are healed. God loves our faith in Him. Take this book and learn to stay in the dance with Jesus because it is His dance, and He wants to lead us, to take our mourning and turn it into joy.

Bibliography

"21 Years Lyrics by Tobymac 2020." 2022. Song-texte.Co. 2022. https://songtexte.co/en/tobymac-21-years-lyrics-1769b8.

Butler, Trent C., editor. 1991a. "Obedience." In *Holman Bible Dictionary*. https://www.studylight.org/dictionaries/eng/hbd/o/obedience.html.

———. 1991b. "Yoke." In *Holman Bible Dictionary*. https://www.studylight.org/dictionaries/eng/hbd/y/yoke.html.

FIRM Staff. 2020. "Crossing the Jordan River and Its Spiritual Significance." FIRM: Fellowship of Israel Related Ministries. 2020. https://firmisrael.org/learn/crossing-jordan-river-spiritual-significance/.

Hagin, Kenneth. 2011. *Following God's Plan for Your Life*. Electronic. Faith Library Publications.

"Holy Spirit Power." 2022. The Family International. 2022. https://www.thefamilyinternational.org/en/faith-foundations/the-basics/holy-spirit-power/.

Lewis, C.S. 2002. *The Great Divorce*. HarperCollins (First published 1945).

"Lookin' for Love by Johnny Lee." 2022. AZLyrics. 2022. https://www.azlyrics.com/lyrics/johnnylee/lookin-forlove.html.

"Quote by Eleanor Roosevelt." 2022. BrainyQuote. 2022. https://www.brainyquote.com/quotes/eleanor_roosevelt_121157.

Reference Staff Writer. 2020. "What Is the Biblical Meaning of the Word 'Restoration'?" Reference. 2020. https://www.reference.com/world-view/biblical-meaning-word-restoration-436ed0eb2e3b3d0c.

"Rest." 2022. In *Merriam-Webster Online Dictionary.* Merriam-Webster, Inc. https://www.merriam-webster.com/dictionary/rest.

Saad, Lydia. 2017. "Record Few Americans Believe Bible Is Literal Word of God." Gallup, Inc. 2017. https://news.gallup.com/poll/210704/record-few-americans-believe-bible-literal-word-god.aspx.

Spurgeon, Charles Haddon. 2017. "God's Estimate of Time." The Spurgeon Center and Midwest-

ern Baptist Theological Seminary. 2017. https://
www.spurgeon.org/resource-library/sermons/
gods-estimate-of-time/#flipbook/.

Strong, James. 1890a. "Condemnation." In *Strong's Exhaustive Concordance of the Bible*. New York: Abingdon Press.

———. 1890b. "Convict." In *Strong's Exhaustive Concordance of the Bible*. New York: Abingdon Press.

Tozer, A.W. 2016. *How to Be Filled with the Holy Spirit*. Reprint. Moody Publishers.

"What Is a Playbook in Football? Definition and Meaning." 2022. SportsLingo. 2022. https://www.sportslingo.com/sports-glossary/p/playbook/.